M~y~

B~est~

L~ifestyle~

The Complete Guide To Building Your Dream Life,
Becoming Your Best Self, And Living Life To The Fullest

ELFRIEDE A.

Diamond
Outcome

DISCLAIMER

My best lifestyle book; the very book you are reading at this moment, is a guide to creating the life of your dreams. It serves as a manual or blueprint for achieving everything you desire in life. In other words, this is a playbook to guide you as you work towards achieving your dreams. This book can be your guide, compass, map, navigation, life plan, to-do list, sense of organization, structure, order, path, reference, diary, journal, and secret weapon.

In this guide, I share my tested-and-true, perfected model for successfully creating your dream life with you. It is a highly simple, yet very in-depth process that is waiting for you in the upcoming chapters. While creating My Best Lifestyle: The Book, I compiled my hard-earned wisdom, accumulated through personal experience, as well as what I have learned through other highly effective references.

Before you start, I want you to know that you do not have to do everything this book suggests as exactly as they are written. They are, as the name suggests, suggestions to guide you to create your dream life most effectively. Most of the advice can be altered to suit your specific needs or capabilities. Even if you do not want to practice every single step exactly as it is written, you can still be able to achieve the results you want or at least some of them. Creating your best lifestyle is a process, so it is completely understandable to start smaller and build up over time based on your needs.

Please, note that I'm not licensed to practice psychiatry, psychology or counselling. My advice is based on life experiences, personal philosophies and personal research, and is not intended or recommended to be used in replacement of psychological or psychiatric counselling. This advice is provided with the understanding that if legal or other assistance is required, the service of a competent professional should be sought.

DEDICATION

To all the day dreamers.

ACKNOWLEDGEMENT

I am full of gratitude for the readers of this book who have chosen to give themselves the best transformation they can, and trusted me to help them achieve it. I am thankful for my trainers and team members who have helped me to put this book together. I am blessed to live a life of wonderful experiences that made it possible for me to write this book.

TABLE OF CONTENTS

INTRODUCTION

Remember when you were a kid, dreaming about who you wanted to be when you grew up. Remember all the things you wanted to own. Remember all the amazing ideas you had about how your life was going to turn out. Maybe you wanted to be rich. Maybe you wanted to be famous. Maybe you wanted to be powerful, or happy, or maybe you wanted it all for yourself. Did you achieve it all? Now let's come back to who you are at the moment, the person you thought you would be when you grew up... Did all of your dreams come true? Did you get the money you wanted, the education you wanted, the dream boy/girl, the house, the cars you wanted? Or, did you have to grow up to acquire mature, more attainable dreams at the expense of giving up your deepest desires? Well, it's not just you. How many of us can truly say that we are living our dream lives?

The truth is, a lot of people are not living their dream lives because they think it is too late to live their dream life. As they get older, life happens, they stop believing in their dreams, and believing in themselves. People often get discouraged as they come to a certain age and realize that they have failed to achieve their dreams, fallen behind the timeline they had in their head, and often give up altogether. For example, so many people thought that they would grow up to be rich and famous, but how many people really became rich and famous when they grow up? Surely, some of these people who did not achieve their dreams are now living with regrets and resentments, but think of the reasons why that happened. What stopped them from achieving their dreams? Whose fault was it that they were unable to achieve them? Is this you? Well, I have good news for you! It is not the end of your story.

I want you to know that as long as you are alive, you still have enough time to achieve your dreams. Here are a few things I want you to realize: adversity does not define your life story. Challenges are nothing but learning opportunities. Adopting the proper mindset and methods will take you to your dream life. This book is your call to action and guide to change your story. I want you to live in your prime, and I am willing to help you with that.

I want you to wake up every day, excited about your life, excited about everything that the new day holds, from this point onward. As human beings, what differentiates us from the rest of the animal kingdom is our need to find and create meaning in our lives. We want to be our best selves, we want to feel satisfied with our life, we want to find happiness. We crave a sense of fulfilment, and we desire to be proud of the life we have created. We want to be mindful about everything we do and only want to love all of our actions. We want to live our life to the fullest. We want to have achievements and be proud of them. We want our dreams to match our lifestyle. We do not only want to connect with ourselves but we also want to connect with the others around us. We want to feel appreciated. We want to feel important. We want to inspire others. We want to help make a difference in the world. In other words, we want to be a part of something bigger than ourselves. This is how we humans are built and this is a good thing knowing what we truly want so we can go after it. This is called living your best lifestyle. Are you ready for it?

What is living your best lifestyle?
Living your best lifestyle means to live your life authentically and unapologetically, in the best way possible. This means not losing your true self and using your most precious qualities to simply maximize your experience on this earth. It

is pretty simple, right? In the end, who wouldn't want to live their best lifestyle?

"My goal is to build a life I don't need a vacation from." -Rob Hill Sr.

You are an extraordinary individual. The choice of living your best life is entirely up to you. Your best lifestyle will mirror your best qualities. It will consist of what makes your heart beat faster and will be suited to the meaning you put behind what living your best lifestyle looks like to you. Living your best lifestyle means getting satisfaction through the one life that you get. It means to live your life in full capacity.

Living your life up to your fullest potential requires choosing to take steps towards your best life every day instead of delaying it to a distant future.

Why is living your best lifestyle important?
Living your best lifestyle will ensure that your life is filled with happiness and fulfilment. The overall satisfaction that you get out of your life will be more maximized than to live an ordinary lifestyle. The purpose is to make you feel satisfied with your life both while living it and at the end of it.

Now that you know why you should be living your best lifestyle, let's talk about how to know if you're already living your best lifestyle.

Signs you are living your best lifestyle
Some ways to know that you're living your best lifestyle are:
1. You are going for the things you want in life
2. You are letting go of limiting beliefs
3. You know your priorities
4. You appreciate the life you have

5. You practice self-care
6. You say 'YES' a lot
7. You say no to things that don't add value to you
8. You have goals or achievements
9. You do not fear change
10. You are staying true to yourself
11. You are joyful
12. You feel fulfilled
13. You feel a sense of flow in your daily activities

The idea of your best lifestyle might sound vague and shallow, but it's far more important than you might think. I'll explain it to you. What exactly happens when you don't live your best lifestyle?

Consequences of not living your best lifestyle
When you choose to settle for a life that isn't your best lifestyle, you experience:
1. Lack of fulfilment
2. Lack of excitement
3. Lack of peace
4. Comparison
5. Confusion
6. Lack of energy or motivation
7. Feeling stuck
8. Lack of growth

Most people aren't satisfied with their lives but aren't doing anything about it. By reading this book, you're already ahead of the majority. It means that you care more about your life and you're taking the necessary steps to give yourself the best life possible. You're on a path to greatness, and that's better than I can say of most people.

Excuses people give for not living their best lifestyle (and the truth).

Over time, I've heard many excuses for why a lot of people have given up on pursuing their dreams. Below you can find a glimpse of the list and the truths about their excuses:

- They do not know that it is still possible. The truth is you can start at any time.
- They have an outmoded definition of success. The truth is they're wrong and don't know it.
- They are too busy running the treadmill of life. The truth is they're spending their life the wrong way.
- They have failed before. The truth is failure isn't the end of the road.
- People have told them to not follow their passion. The truth is people might have been wrong.
- They do not have the confidence. Truth is confidence can be learned.
- They think they do not have the money. The truth is your budget for what's important to you.
- They do not have a plan. Truth is, a plan is easy to create.
- They claim to not have time to pursue their dreams. The truth is if something is important to you, you will make time for it.
- They believe that their goals are too big. The truth is, if you can dream it then you can
- achieve it.
- They think that life is hard. The truth is if they put in more effort into the right places, it will work out in the end.
- They think that pursuing their goals is risky. The truth is, what's truly risky is spending
- the rest of your life not living the way you really want to live.

- They think good things only come to those who wait. Truth is only so much will just
- come to you out of nowhere. If you want to have it all, you have to work for it.
- They think they will fail. The truth is they don't realize that every outcome in life is either a win or a learning opportunity. Failure only happens when you do not try or you give up.
- They think that they cannot do it. Truth is that they cannot do it YET.

Trust me, I know what it's like to feel hopeless. Let me tell you my story.

MY TRANSFORMATION STORY

The thing about me is I've always been an introvert, so I practically live in my head. I spent a lot of my childhood thinking. I was trying to find out who I was. I was very curious to know what my life's purpose was and where I wanted to go in life. I found myself naturally drawn to learning about the mind process, what constitutes a good life, how to be successful, personal development and psychology in general. What I always knew was that I wanted to be happy and successful. As I grew up, around 12 years old, I decided to start writing down my thoughts. I wanted to see my thoughts on paper, so I started keeping a journal. I mostly wrote about the things I wanted to acquire, like my dream home and cars. At the time, I did not fully understand what I was doing, neither did I know where I was going with it.

In Nigeria, where I grew up, I didn't know anybody at my age that was doing anything like this. The closest thing I knew was keeping a diary. But there I was, making future plans, at 12 years old. It was simply what I felt the need to do. As I did it, I noticed that it added value to my life, so I simply continued doing it. As a teenager, my need for clarity became more prominent. This was the age when everyone wanted to be cool and fit in. I didn't want to be like everyone else. I wanted real happiness. I often dreamt of freedom.

When I was 15 years old, I experienced a period of severe anxiety and depression. I felt anxiety because I did not know who I was or where my life was going. I needed a sense of direction and something to live for. I was depressed because of some personal issues I was dealing with. My depression made me lose all sense of interest in daily activities. In fact, I was having suicidal thoughts.

I overcame depression with self-awareness, self-acceptance, self-love, self-care, and life planning in my journal. This is why I believe so much in life planning and self-knowledge. Today, I credit my progress to it. My journal reduced my anxiety and depression. My life was chaotic and my journal seemed to be my only escape and hope for the future. I began journaling more intensely. I took a lot of personality quizzes to increase my self-awareness. I enjoyed knowing what things suited me. I wrote everything I wanted to do in my journal. I became more focused. I started working on my dreams and goals, and on my action plans for reaching these goals. Anytime I felt lost or confused, I would refer to my journal to recalibrate. It kept me focused and made me aware that my life had a purpose.

After a couple of years, seeing how my life had improved, I realized that life planning was a genius idea. I noticed that I became more organized and focused. I found myself ticking off goals one by one. I was blossoming into the woman I always wanted to be. I was genuinely happy. My mates wondered about me and wanted to be like me. Self-knowledge and life planning was my secret.

As an adult, I felt like I had changed my life so I wanted to change other people's lives, too. I felt like it was my gift to the world. I wanted to own it, share it, market it, transform it, grow it, and more. I was proud of myself. So, I decided to write this book to share what I've learned. I hope I can help you become happier and fulfilled. The advice in this book is a more sophisticated version of what I started doing when I was 12 years old. I, personally, remember starting with only keeping a journal and becoming very happy and confident with life. As I got older, I discovered and developed other methods of achieving my ideal life.

You can rise from anything. You can completely recreate yourself. Nothing is permanent but nothing is going to change if you do not change. You are not stuck. You have choices. You can think of new thoughts. You can learn something new. You can create new habits. All that matters is that you decide today and never look back.

The chapters in this book are divided into distinct sections that serve their own purpose. Each chapter is a different step in the process of achieving your dream life.

In Chapter 1 (My Life Purpose), you will learn about your life purpose. What is it, why it matters and how to find yours.

In Chapter 2 (My Life Mindset), you will learn about the mindset that is holding you back and the new mindset that you need to adopt to create your dream life.

In Chapter 3 (My Life Vision), you will learn to visualize your dream life and how to manifest it into becoming your reality.

In Chapter 4 (My Life Design), you will learn how to decide and set goals for the things that you want in each area of your life.

In Chapter 5 (My Life Blueprint), you will learn the steps to make your goals your actual reality. You will also create plans that you can start working on immediately.

In Chapter 6 (My Lifestyle), you will learn how to navigate through life the best way that you can. You will learn about the tips and techniques to maintain a dream life and become the best version of yourself.

Finally, is the conclusion of the book.

CHAPTER ONE

MY LIFE PURPOSE

L iving your best lifestyle involves living in alignment with your life purpose. So, let me ask you: have you fulfilled yours? Are you on the path to fulfilling yours? How would you feel if you died without fulfilling yours?

Discovering your purpose in life isn't always easy, as I am convinced that the inability to do so is one of the reasons behind the unhappiness of many people. And for many people, for several years, they do nothing but wander from one place to another, from one job to another, from one project to another, in search of what truly satisfies them, which is their life purpose.

WHAT IS YOUR LIFE PURPOSE?
The question "what is your life purpose?" concerns an inner aspect, a personal, profound journey to discover ourselves. Here's the thing about your truest dreams- they never change. Yes, even if the circumstances surrounding your life changes, even if you move on to engage in unbecoming things; your truest dream still remains at the core of your existence. If something is your truest dream, your mission, then it will remain unchanged and unharmed despite the situations and the challenges that life throws at you. It doesn't matter where life takes you, what decisions you make, or where you end up; your truest dream still remains and will be your trigger once you pay attention to it to find expression.

Of the truth, true happiness comes when you start living in alignment with your purpose. However, it is easier said than done. I can help you find the burning fire in your soul. In the end, the most important part of the journey is finding out what makes you feel alive.

"Ten years from now, make sure you can say that you chose your life and didn't settle for it." -Mandy Hale

Your life's purpose is simply your destiny. It is the thing that you were meant to do with your life all along. I believe that the purpose of your life is to fulfil your destiny. On a more religious side, I think that God put you on this earth for at least one reason. That reason or reasons are your destiny or life purpose. I believe that your duty is to discover it and fulfil it.

For some people, they believe their life's purpose is what they've discovered by looking (searching deeply) inward, for others, they think it lies in their responsibilities to their family or friends. Some may seek meaning through spirituality or religion, whereas some may find it in every single aspect of their lives.

Life's purpose is unique for everyone, as everyone's identity will lead to a different path. What's more, one's desires or interests can shift and change throughout life experiences, and yet the essence of the purpose within remains.

There are three key questions you need to reflect upon your life's purpose:
 Who am I?
 Where do I belong?
 When do I feel fulfilled?

THE BENEFITS THAT COME WITH DISCOVERING YOUR PURPOSE IN LIFE
Finding one's life purpose can:

2

- Guide life decisions
- Influence behaviour
- Shape goals
- Offer a sense of direction
- Create meaning
- Help you stay focused
- Make you feel passionate about your goal
- Give your life a sense of clarity
- Make you feel gratified
- Enable you to live a value-based life
- Make you live with integrity
- Encourage trust
- Infuse an element of grace
- Help you find a flow
- Simply make your life even more fun

When you fulfil your destiny, or life purpose, you'll feel truly happy and will positively impact the lives of others around you. Others will feel joy because of you. This is why it is important to stir your potential, discover your vision and realize it.

Mark Twain expressed it perfectly: "The two most important days of our lives are the day we were born and the day we find out why."

Finding your life purpose makes life more meaningful and enjoyable. It yields the fruits of happiness and fulfilment.

FACTORS TO CONSIDER IN DISCOVERING YOUR LIFE PURPOSE
Why am I here?
When you ask yourself this question inwardly you begin to dig in search of the truth about yourself, about life, about

God. This sets your feet on the true path of knowledge and awareness. An important stage of my journey was when I had the sensation of being much more than my "little me". I was reconnecting with my soul and the more I did it, the more I discovered peace in the search for the meaning of my life. Certainly, some of the questions that accompanied me inwardly at that time were questions like: what can I do for others? How can I give the best of myself? This allowed me to open up to a wider vision and project myself towards my true purpose. Since then, I have always tried to understand what my soul's dream was and to find meaning in existence.

The answers to your questions always come, you just have to trust and start asking yourself the "right" questions. Ask and you shall receive.

Does life have a purpose?
Come to think of it, isn't the purpose of life, perhaps, the experience of life itself? The evolution of one's conscience? Sometimes it is not easy to answer certain inner questions because many things are submerged in us and to be able to see within, we should always be "centred."

An important thing to understand is that there is never something wrong or something missing at any moment in your life. By living your life, you are already doing what you should be doing. If you feel an inner urge to change your life and do something else, simply do it. But it will not do you any good to think that your life, at the moment, is not good, just because you don't have all the answers. The present moment is perfect as it is, it is the exact experience you need to have. Accept it (welcome it) and everything will flow much better. On the other hand, there is nothing other than the present. If you live in the present moment, your life purpose will become clearer to you. Live here and now.

Discover your mission

Understanding one's mission could be an important aspect of finding the meaning of one's life. So, what should you do? Listen to your passions, identify your attitudes and talents, and recognize your worth. Stop for a moment and think about what makes you truly happy. Maybe you already know, and then have the courage to follow it. Recognize your value and try to create it for others through your talents. Finding this intent could be a way to move you in the right direction of finding purpose and meaning in life.

But how can I do it?

Start by letting go. Try to let go of the things that don't make you happy, that don't identify with your mind, and accept (or rather welcome) life as it is. Above all, realize that the responsibility of your life is yours. Not guilt, but the power to transform it as you created it. It depends on you.

Find your personal "mission," because it will give meaning to your life. Everyone has to make their own path, as each of us have our own sense of existence. You can discover your personal mission by asking yourself several questions: What are the things you stand for? What great things do you want to see more of in this world? How do you plan to make them happen? What are the unique and valuable things you have to offer this world?

Look at this diagram on ikigai, meaning life purpose:

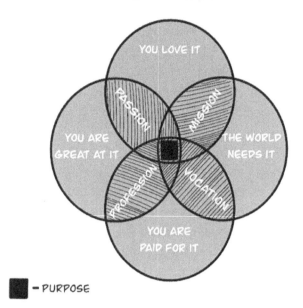

■ — PURPOSE

Everything is perfect

If you have the vision that everything in life is perfect as it is, then you probably understand that there is always a reason why things happen. Nothing happens by chance. This is how it works. Understanding that everything is perfect now opens you to a positive outlook on life. You are able to accept situations without judging them and you do not create unnecessary pain in your life.

This attitude also leads you to develop positive thinking. How powerful thoughts have now also been demonstrated by science but if you start experiencing them in your life, you will really realize how much power you have to transform them. Everything is perfect like this. Don't try to change things out, if anything, try to change yourself. It is not what happens in reality that is important, but what happens inside you.

I know it may seem like something not easy to accept. When you hear the phrase "everything is perfect" thoughts immediately come to mind like: "war, famine, violence... how can everything be perfect?" I understand you but don't judge. The concept that "everything is perfect" does not mean that everything is beautiful or that it is as you would like it to be. It is not important what happens outside, or what is happening around you, but rather focus on what happens inside you, because that is where you can act. Beauty is like happiness, it is always there. It is up to your eyes whether you are able to see it or not.

"Everything has beauty but not everyone can see it." - Confucius

5 Laws Of Life

This concept is explained to us by the spiritual laws of the Indian tradition (which are still taught in India today) which allow us to understand the meaning of life even better. As if the law of Karma were not enough, with these spiritual laws, it is even clearer that randomness does not exist, but rather everything happens according to perfection that does not admit alternatives of what happens or the people we meet or whoever leaves our life, are exactly what is supposed to happen.

- The person who arrives is the right person
- What happens is the only thing that could have happened
- The moment in which it happens is the right moment
- When something ends, it ends
- Suffering is okay too

Have you ever thought about why we find ourselves reflecting on the meaning of life especially when we go through moments of suffering? These periods of life force us to stop and meditate deeply. At that moment we take another step in the path of personal growth. Every suffering, every disease has the gift of enriching and improving us. If we discover the true inner cause of our pain, we have the opportunity to transform and evolve. In these moments, it's as if life tells us: "Hey, you do not love yourself enough!" - In fact, when we don't have enough love for ourselves, we don't have it for others and for life.

So, even these moments of suffering are fundamental because we are helping to understand we must learn to love truly, love unconditionally; perhaps this is the meaning of life! Love others and yourself as you are, don't judge yourself, don't feel wrong because there is nothing wrong, everything is perfect! Love is the vibration of life, it is who we are. It is life itself. Everything is love.

"One sees clearly only with the heart." - Antoine De Saint-Exupéry

My Sense Of Life
What are we all looking for? How to be happy, in peace, and in good health... isn't it? Personally, to achieve true inner peace, I went through a lot of suffering (like almost everyone). I have experienced that the happiness that comes from material things is temporary and superficial. The inner one, on the other hand, is more permanent and is not conditioned from the outside.
Happiness is a state of being! You can't have happiness, but you can be happy. But to do this you need to learn not to be a slave to your own mind and choose to be. There is also another aspect that concerns one's sense of life, which is to understand why we are here, embodied in a human body.

Gradually in the great game of life, we discover what our soul has come to learn and thus continue on the great journey back to "home".

My purpose in this life, before "returning," is to help improve the world compared to how I found it (which in the end is a job to improve myself) trying never to create suffering for me and others. This should be your purpose too.

HOW TO FIND YOUR LIFE PURPOSE
Finding your purpose in life isn't always easy, but it's a vital part of life. That is why I wrote this book. You read my story and you know how I came to write this book. My goal is to show anyone who feels defeated, lost, and surrendered that alternatives exist and a happy life is within everyone's reach.

No matter what your idea of happiness is, you should still discover your life purpose. You should make decisions that align with who you are and where you want to go. To do this, start asking the right questions. One above all: what is the purpose of my life?

If you haven't found it yet, read these 8 questions and answer honestly. These are questions that I asked myself at different moments in my life, and they helped me in discovering the coordinates of my happiness.

1. What do you love to do?
The very first question you should ask yourself if you want to understand what your life purpose is, is about what you love. Love is the basis of everything, love is happiness.

What do you like to do? What makes you smile? What activities do you do without experiencing any discomfort, boredom, or pain? In my case, journaling was one of them: I could write all day and every day, and I would never get tired. When I realized I had this healthy "addiction," I realized that it could become the purpose of my occupation and personal life. So, I decided to turn that passion into a way of supporting myself and the other lives out there.

Think about what you love to do, compile a list of activities you enjoy, and study it for a while in silence and solitude. Chances are that on that list is your Ikigai, your life purpose.

2. If money wasn't a problem, what job would you like to do? This is a key question, because work, whether you like it or not, will take up a large part of your life. Work is what you will do for several hours a day, most of your week, for several decades of your life. Not enough support is given to young people in choosing a job, when in reality it would be essential to teach them that finding the right job means getting very close to their happiness.

If you had a choice, what job would you like to do? The answer is really important. You may want a traditional job or a job that gives you a lot of free time. A safe job or an adrenaline pumping job. A job that leaves you space and time for your passions or a job that is your passion. Find a job you love and you'll never have to work again.

3. What are the happiest memories you have?
Stop and take a minute to think about the best moments of your life. Bring out the memories and dive into the past to relive those fragments of happiness. Watch that short memorial movie and realize that your life purpose is right there, in the midst of those memories. On the other hand, think about how nice it would be to live only moments like

those that you consider the happiest of your existence; doesn't that mean that you have found your purpose in life? In the end, that purpose is always about your happiness.

4. When do you feel at home?
We grow up convinced that "home" is the place where we were born but the concept of "home" goes beyond what is written on our identity card.

Feeling at home is not just a matter of place. "Home" is a mix of sensations that you receive when you are in a certain place, but especially when you are with certain people. You feel at home looking into the eyes of the man or woman you love, having a nice time hanging out with your best and true friends, chatting with your ever listening and attentive counsellor. Think about it: when did you feel at home? Who or what gave you that feeling? You can find the purpose of your life by answering these two questions. You can have many goals in your existential journey but you certainly want to be able to feel at home.

5. Think about the people you respect: why do you admire them?
People are a source of inspiration who can help you find the coordinates of your happiness.

Think about the people you respect: why do you look at them with admiration? What are the features you appreciate? Why would you want to look like them (while still being yourself)? Answer these questions and you will easily find your life purpose. Don't be ashamed to take cues from those you respect or even ask them for life and professional advice, people can be amazing resources. Put your ego aside and humbly analyze the success stories around you. This makes it easier to understand the right direction to take in your life.

6. What are you good at?

What are your natural talents? Your talents are the things you do with less effort than others. Think of things you're naturally drawn to. Think of the things you do that make you lose track of time when you perform those activities. I want you to think about it for a moment and when you find something you're really good at, you should consider dedicating yourself, body and soul.

If you find something that comes easy and natural to you, you will have a less tiring life. Your life will become more enjoyable for you. You will feel more motivated to become your best. The formula is this: if it doesn't make you unhappy and if you can do it well, then it could be your life purpose.

Along with natural talents, think of some skills you can develop. Some skills can help you utilize your talents more effectively.

7. If no one judged you, what would you do with your life?

A question that few answer honestly. Imagine that you have moved to the other side of the world. You are alone and nobody knows you. They don't even know your name. How would you reprogram your life? Would you look for work in the same field you work in now? Would you have the same hobbies? Would you organize your days the same way? Would you behave differently?

If you answer these questions with excitement from the thought of a completely different life from the one you have now, then there is a problem. The purpose of your existence lies not in what you do now but in what you would like to do if no one judged you. If so, ask yourself another question: do you want to continue living your life to keep the expectations of others, or do you want to live simply happy?

8. What are the changes you would like to see in the world? Happiness is not a one-way street. Happiness is an exchange: you can't get it if you don't learn to give some. From my point of view, this discourse also applies very well to the search for one's purpose in life: do not think one-sidedly, thinking only of your personal fulfilment.

Do not search far for your purpose. It's right within you! Follow your most persistent and deepest thoughts, therein your vision lies, the things you desire to see.

Think broadly and universally: Do you want to make sense of your journey on this earth? Then try to think about what you could do to concretely leave it in a better state than the one in which you met it. There are those who find their purpose in helping others, those who want to save the planet from pollution, those who live to reduce waste, some to save people who are lost, others to share positivity and bring a few more smiles. The purpose of your life is also and above all in what you can give, not only in what you can receive. What are the changes you want to see in the world?

Answer this question and remember what Gandhi said: "Be the change you want to see in the world." -Mahatma Gandhi

CHAPTER TWO

MY LIFE MINDSET

There is a trait of your mentality that can deeply affect your life: from study to career, passing from sport to relationships. In this chapter, we will see in detail what it is and how you develop a winning mindset.

WHAT IS YOUR LIFE MINDSET?
By simple definition, mindset is the way things are conceived to a person, a group, a community, etc. It is the mental structure of an individual towards life. It is your attitude or point of view concerning a subject.

WHY YOU SHOULD DEVELOP YOUR LIFE MINDSET
Maintaining the right mindset is more important than you might think. I want you to understand that your mind is a tool, a controllable tool, that affects your performance, and it is completely possible to reprogram it based on your beliefs. If you believe that you can achieve a thing, you will be more likely to pursue it, put in your best effort, and therefore become more likely to achieve it. But, if you don't believe you can achieve a thing, you reduce your chances of achieving it, or might not even bother. This theory is based just on what you believe.

HOW TO DEVELOP YOUR LIFE MINDSET
To develop your mindset, first you need to discover the thinking patterns that hold you back, then use techniques to change them into empowering thoughts. I'll explain it to you further.

SPHERES OF CONTROL, INFLUENCE AND CONCERN

I want you to understand just how much power you have over your own life. The reason is because I want you to also understand that the choices you pick either take you forward or backwards. You have the power to change your circumstances. Every event that is ever happening in your life falls into one of 3 spheres:

- Control: The things you can control (an example is what you eat)
- Influence: The things you cannot control but can influence (an example is the way a person thinks of you)
- Concern: The things you can neither control nor influence, presently and at all times (an example is your genes)

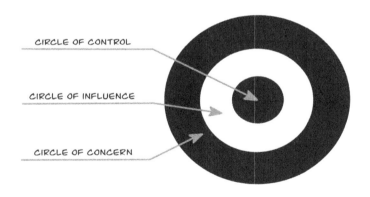

This is the reason you should make the most of what you can control and influence, and worry less about what you cannot control since you cannot do anything about them anyway. There is no point in worrying about things that are beyond your control because worrying only steals your joy, it does not make the problem go away. Since there are some aspects of your life that you can control/influence to create your ideal life, why not use them to make your life what you desire it to be?

Circling back to my initial point, your mind is a tool that you have control over, or at least can influence. The way you think, feel, react, act, etc are all your choice. That choice is power. That choice can make or break you. That choice can change negative to positive, and positive to negative. Choose your response wisely.

Every external event that takes place in our life calls for one of 3 internal reactions:
1. How we choose to view the situation.
2. How we choose to react to the situation.
3. How we choose to allow the situation to influence our life afterward

"Our problems cannot be solved at the same level of thinking we were at when we created them." -Albert Einstein

Let me ask you: are you going to let a traumatic event hold you back or motivate you? It's all in how you choose to respond. Once you implement a positive mindset to influence how you react to any life event, it is possible to notice the advantages and proceed with them.

You should look on the bright side and believe in yourself to be able to move forward from any situation in life, and it will be easier to do this if you implement a positive lifestyle. Believe! That's it. Believe in miracles. Believe that anything is possible. Clear up your mind, remove all obstacles and blockages, let go of all feelings of fears, doubts, insecurities, and negativity. Good things never result from negativity. Negative thoughts lead to negative results. Watch those thoughts.

This model describes the power of thoughts:

LIMITING BELIEFS

"Your beliefs become your thoughts, your thoughts become your words, your words become your actions, your actions

My Life Mindset

become your habits, your habits become your values, and your values become your destiny." -Mahatma Gandhi

The moment you make statements like "I cannot do that because..." anything that comes after "because" is a self-limiting thought. A self-limiting thought is a belief you have that makes you underestimate your abilities. It is a pattern of negative thought that discourages you. This consequently prevents you from reaching your true potential.

Examples of self-limiting beliefs
A self-limiting statement usually starts like this:
"I do not..."
"I cannot..."
"I must not..."
"I am not..."

You reap what you sow. When you speak negativity into your life, life gives you negativity back. When you speak positivity into your life, life gives you positivity in return. It is as simple as that. Do not give power to things that you do not wish to invite into your life. You give power to negative thoughts by thinking of them, imagining them, expecting them, worrying about them, and so on. By feeding them your energy and mental space, you manifest them into your reality.

The same way it's possible to manifest negative thoughts, you can manifest positive thoughts. Give your attention to positivity, blessings, abundance, wealth, health, success, happiness, and other good things that you want to attract into your life. This is precisely why you should focus on the positive. Give your energy to positive things as you create your reality. The way you talk to yourself, the way you think; all impact how your life events turn out. So, be mindful of how

18

you talk to yourself, adopt positive self-talk to channel positive outcomes from your life.

POSITIVE SELF-TALK

How you communicate with yourself sets the tone for your day, and even life. As I went through in the previous section, you need to adopt a positive approach when talking to yourself to optimize the outcome of your situation. This is where positive self-talk comes into play.

To be able to adopt positive self-talk, it is essential to pay attention to the patterns you use when referring to yourself to see the tone you are choosing more often. When you pay closer attention to how you speak to yourself, you notice the errors that you might be making and can start making proactive changes. These changes will help you deal with life's challenges more efficiently.

What Is Positive Self-Talk?

Positive self-talk, as suggested, is simply the flip of negative talk. It's not about narcissism or misleading yourself into speculation about wrong things. It's about progressively giving yourself some self-sympathy and comprehension for what your identity is and what you are experiencing. Simply put, positive self-talk is aimed at loving yourself and saying things that encourage positivity. It means talking to yourself positively.

Switch Up Your Internal Dialogue

Watch those dialogues that you have with yourself, in your head. They might sound like self-doubt, nagging, or even make you feel like a victim. It's easier to be pessimistic than optimistic. In fact, optimism might sound like *you're living in the clouds*. This is a normal thought, but you shouldn't cultivate it. You should stop and change it as soon as you notice it.

Childhood Programming

You are not responsible for the programming you received in childhood. However, as an adult, you are one hundred percent responsible for your current mindset. Think of the first time someone told you something negative about yourself. Most likely, you were very young. Your loved ones might have knowingly or unknowingly ruined your dreams. Sometimes, just observing the way your loved ones live can alter your thinking. For example, because your mother divorced your father might make you feel hopeless about marriage. Some of these passed down ideas are outdated and untrue. Let them go and form new, empowering beliefs. Rewrite your own life story. Give yourself a happy ending.

Forgive Yourself For Your Mistakes

No human is always good or always bad. Stop letting mistakes, shame or regret dictate your life. Forgive yourself. You cannot change the past but you can learn from your mistakes and grow. Afterall, you're only human.

I want you to understand that a bad experience is not a bad life and that your energy is precious. You should let go of every negative thing you ever heard and have been told about yourself. They're not true! Your dreams are not too big. You are not too old. You are not too young. You are not stupid. It's not out of reach. People have their reasons for saying these kinds of things to you. They might have psychological issues themselves. Even if more than one person has said it to you, it does not mean that these things are true. I'm saying to you: your dreams are still possible. Reset your mind, accept your blessings, accept your growth.

Accept this opportunity and believe me, amazing things are coming your way. Let go of things that no longer serve you. Phrases like "I cannot," or "but..." are used to make excuses.

Challenge Your Negative Self-Beliefs

Question your negative thoughts, prove them wrong, and replace them with empowering thoughts. Practice your newfound empowerment until it becomes ingrained in you. Change your negative self-talk to something more positive like "I can improve next time," or "I decide to gain from my slip-ups, and not be kept down by them." Align your mindset with the life you desire to create. Dispose of outdated beliefs because they do not serve you, neither do they encourage you to accomplish a positive goal. Shift fear and nervous thoughts to excitement and enthusiasm.

Instead of having negative thoughts after a bad experience, ask yourself: "What is this situation trying to teach me? You should get into the habit of asking yourself this question every time you have a negative experience. This is just one way of reframing dysfunctional beliefs.

REFRAME DYSFUNCTIONAL BELIEFS

Changing dysfunctional beliefs is all about changing your point of view, or perspective. It is about thinking bigger and better, instead of limited and difficult. Let's go through some examples of dysfunctional beliefs and how we can reframe them into positive ones:

Dysfunctional belief: I can only be happy if I am successful.
Reframe: My true happiness comes from designing a life that works for me. Dysfunctional belief: It is too late to have my dream life.
Reframe: It is never too late to design a life I love.
Dysfunctional belief: I have to find the one right idea.

21

Reframe: I want a lot of ideas so that I can explore any number of possibilities for my future.

Dysfunctional belief: I need to figure out my best possible life I can think of, make a plan, and then execute it.

Reframe: There are multiple great lives (and plans) within me, and I get to select which one I want to build my way towards.

Dysfunctional belief: I have finished designing my life; the hard work is done and the result will be great.

Reframe: I can never finish designing my life because my life is a joyous and never-ending design project. I can always re-design, change my mind, change directions, add new ideas, and more.

Activity

Think of some dysfunctional beliefs that you have and reframe them

Look at this example. Ryan says "We only have 30 days to adjust ourselves."

Bad news: A lot can change in 30 days.

Good news: A lot can change in 30 days.

Both statements say the same thing but one of them is perceived as good news, while the other one is perceived as bad news. Do you know why? It only depends on your PERSPECTIVE. 30 days can be full of great events or devastating events, depending on your point of view. You can choose to view your experience as negative or positive, and that's the way it will be for you. This is exactly what your belief system can do. The way you view an experience is important.

For example, instead of saying "that experience turned my life upside down," you can say "that experience made me grow." I know this is easier said than done, but the longer you practice your new belief, the harder it will be for your belief to leave you. True, beliefs that you have held for a long time are harder to change but can still be changed. As you get older, your beliefs will change naturally. Release believes that no longer serve you or hold you back in life. Your mind needs to work towards your favour, not against you. A positive outlook is encouraging. A growth mindset is a way to develop positive self-talk.

GROWTH MINDSET

One way of training your mind to work for your benefit is to adopt a growth mindset. If you have a growth mindset, it means you would rather take advantage of situations to improve yourself and your life, rather than let situations get the best of you. A growth mindset means that you see every situation as an inspiration rather than a setback. A growth mindset encourages the ability to grow, and develop new skills and talents as you grow, through effort. It favors cultivating new skills and abilities instead of ending growth at your natural talents. You need a growth mindset to grow and thrive, so naturally, it is essential to living a successful life.

People who adopt a growth mindset into their lives desire to become the best version of themselves. They want to add more effort into making themselves better. They continue to grow and improve. They are better at coping with failures because they see challenges as opportunities to learn or try something different, instead of seeing failures as end zones. A growth mindset is also an abundance mindset.

Here are some examples of a growth mindset thinking style:
- Everyone starts from somewhere
- A lot of successful people have failed before

- I need to put in more effort
- If I do not try, I have already failed
- I accept my responsibility
- I am always looking for the meanings and lessons in all situations that can help me become my best self

On the opposite side of the growth mindset resides people with a fixed mindset. A person with a fixed mindset believes things like skills and talents are only obtained when a person is born, or that skills and talents become locked into a person at a certain time. The fixed mindset person favours natural abilities at the expense of cultivated abilities. They believe that you either have it or you do not. They do not encourage effort. A fixed mindset is also a scarcity mindset.

Examples of the fixed mindset thinking are:
"I am not good enough"
"It is not my fault"
"I do not want to take this risk"
"I will probably fail"
"I am not naturally good at this, I should just quit"
I've provided some examples of how you can reframe a fixed mindset into a growth mindset:
Fixed: I was born with no rhythm, so I do not dance.
Growth: I know that dancing is not my natural talent, but I will become better with practice.
Fixed: I am never able to keep my emails organized.
Growth: I am going to try new techniques to keep my emails organized.
Fixed: Nothing is going right. It seems to me that today is just going to be one of those days.
Growth: Today has not been going well so far, but I can learn from my errors and prepare for a better tomorrow.

How To Develop A Growth Mindset

Now that you know what a growth mindset is, how do you develop it? Here are some steps to assist you:

STEP 1: Develop awareness of your fixed mindset
Be aware of your fixed mindset's voice. It sounds like it is warning you or trying to keep you safe, but it is just limiting or stopping you all together. For example, it might be said things like:
"This is not for me"
"I do not belong here"
"I am not good enough"

STEP 2: Do not give in
You need to remember that you do not have to listen to that voice. You always have a choice of how you receive and respond.

STEP 3: Actively choose the positive route
Change your perspective from a fixed (lacking) mindset to a growth (abundance) mindset. Talk back (not literally) to the fixed mindset's voice with a growth mindset's voice. Correct the fixed mindset's statements. For example, if the fixed mindset's voice says you aren't capable of doing something, talk back to it by saying that you can learn.

STEP 4: Take growth mindset actions
Be active with your growth mindset-thinking. Take actions towards getting what you want. Do your research for the steps to getting what you want and start preparing yourself for it. For example, ask yourself: what could you do differently next time? What steps will you take? What can you do immediately to increase your chances of getting what you want in the future?

I want to end this chapter on this note: It is time to live your truth and claim your greatness. Make use of all your wisdom, experiences, and passion. You should be living life on your terms. You should be mindful of everything you do. When you wake up in the morning, you should feel enthusiastic about the activities of the day. You should not live anyone else's dream life, live yours. The fact is that if you don't live your dream, someone will use you to live theirs. At the end of the day, you are the person that will be left with the result of YOUR LIFE. You are the one who is going to live it every day. Don't you want a life that you are proud of? You should not have to settle forever. You only have one life, optimize your chances of success.

CHAPTER THREE

MY LIFE VISION

K nowing what you want is one of the first steps to getting it. An amazing thing about your mind is when you give it a vision, it helps you find it. In this chapter, we will be working on creating your life's vision and how to make that vision a reality.

"The only thing worse than being blind is having sight but no vision." -Helen Keller

I just heard you say: "Elfriede, in the first chapter of this book you talked about purpose and now you are talking about vision; is there any difference?" Yes, they are distinctly different and I'm going to shed light on that now.

The Difference Between Vision And Purpose
Vision and purpose are two words that can sometimes be confusing, although there are distinct differences between the two. Vision can simply be defined as a mental image of the future. In business management, vision refers to the future position of an organizational body. The vision is the pinnacle of the organization's success. On the other hand, purpose refers to a much more specific, quantifiable, and detailed goal. The key difference between vision and purpose is that while the vision may seem far and wide, the purpose is much more specific and achievable. Your ability to envision your future is your evolutionary advantage and it can be developed.

WHAT IS YOUR LIFE VISION?

I have come to this definition of the vision of life. It is a mental image or picture that is created by the power of your imagination, which reflects what your inner desire wants to achieve. Vision is a product of creative imagination and dreams. Your vision will be your guiding star that will guide you towards the right direction in your journey, and keep you on track. A successful person will be able to see their future brightly, in colors, in the smallest detail, as if the future is near. By creating your vision of your best life, you choose a new line for your destiny.

A life vision is a picture that has the aspects of what you want your life to look like. Visualization is the place you build up a distinctive picture in your psyche, of the information you are attempting to make or recollect. Your vision of life serves to be clear about the general lines of your existence, what fits and what does not fit in your life. In this way, if you define your vision of life, you will be able to align everything that is underneath (mission, areas, objectives, projects, etc.) with respect to what you want to achieve. This way, everything is much clearer and easier.

Your vision of life is one of the many ways you have to define how you want your life to be. Your life vision does not need to have a format or a specific way of realizing it. To be clear about your vision, you must be clear about who you want to be. For example, to get an idea of what a fairly short life vision might be, you could approach it as follows: to be a better person day after day, to have a quiet life as a couple and family, and to continue learning the issues that motivate me, as well as to achieve all the personal and professional aspirations that I set out for myself. A vision could be half a page or a whole page. I think that this phrase sums up the idea of life vision very well. Many things are missing, but the vision remains with what is essential for me.

Personal vision: What future do I want to build?
Days go by and many people move without approaching their own goals, feeling that they did nothing yesterday or today. We all know someone who always seems to be full of projects that he never seems to achieve or carry out successfully. Now, why is this happening? And more importantly, what can you do to achieve a different result?
A lack of personal vision causes this feeling of "doing nothing" or "never getting to where I want to go."

"The only thing worse than being blind is having sight but no vision" -Hellen Keller

You should begin by knowing what personal vision is and what it is used for. Personal vision is a linguistic construction in which you define your own desired future. For example: My personal vision is within 5 years to be an outstanding and recognized professional in my industry, accompanying processes of personal and organizational transformation and maintaining the service values that characterize me. Designing your future using this tool will allow you to plan your actions using personal vision as an orientation to where to go.

One of the keys to a powerful vision is the realism with which it enunciates, communicates, and sustains a reality that is not yet but will undoubtedly be. Listening to the vision, there should be no doubt about what you want to achieve and when it will happen. When writing it, visualize not only what will happen but also how you are going to feel and relate to others in that new reality. Let your mind fly and relate to all the possibilities of your being. We constantly design and redesign ourselves, building your personal vision and mission is the first step to achieve what you set out to do.

To be clear about your vision, you must be clear about who you are
Having a clear vision of life is essential for you to move forward towards your personal productivity. Productivity is not based on doing a lot with little time, but on doing what is important and what brings you closer to your ideal way of life. To be clear about your vision, you must be clear about who we are, what you do, and how you do it, what you would like to do, and how you would like to do it.

Imagine that someone new comes into your life, someone who is very special to you and you would love to impress. Imagine if the person asks you: "where would you like to be in 5 years?" What will your answer be if you want to be totally honest? What answer would you give yourself if you said, "where do I want to be in 5 years?"

If you are still not very clear about who you are, how you are, or what you want, the time has come for you to reflect. You might think at that moment that you don't have time, but you have to make time! It's best to start that reflection now! Leave the less important issues alone and get to work on your own life. Things like work are very important, but life is everything. You should make an effort to advance in your personal development, and your life vision is a crucial step forward. It is a path that we must travel as soon as possible.

WHY YOU NEED A LIFE VISION
1. Guidance: When you have a life vision, it gives you something to work towards. It gives you clarity, so you can

experience your days realizing that you are moving towards what you need, want, and the things that are important to you.

2. Motivation: A life vision tends to be uplifting, and you should make sure it is. If your life vision is boring, you are not going to want to take care of business. Your life vision ought to line up with your values, so you would desire to work towards it. The reason for a life vision exercise or plan is to make an attractive future that causes you to centre your life, and take action!

3. Illumination: A person who has a vision has a higher chance of achieving set goals. Vision helps you take control of your life. Vision is the beacon that illuminates your path and helps you make the right decisions in life, clearly see your future, and supports you in difficult periods of your life.

The vision and its commitment is something like the situation in the mountains, when you throw your backpack on the next ledge above you, knowing that now you need to climb, since all the necessary equipment is already there, at the top. Vision creates strong intrinsic motivation that allows you to overcome fears and obstacles, both external and internal.

HOW TO WRITE YOUR LIFE VISION
To define your vision, it helps to give it a physical reality by writing it down. There are three important rules for writing your vision.

1. Write in the first person.
Whether it's the first person singular, "I," if you're writing for yourself, or the first-person plural "we" if you share a common vision with someone else. You should make your vision your

own. If you write "He", it is an impersonal form. It detaches you from it.

2. Write in the affirmative form.
A vision does not involve "not." Your unconscious does not know how to read it, it does not know how to integrate it. The "not" risks being realized by your unconscious mind because your mind picks up everything you say and makes it your reality, without realizing what you're rejecting. For example, don't write "I don't want to be in a bad situation", but rather, "I want to be in a good situation."

3. Write in the present tense.
Writing in the present is essential. This is essential. If you write it in the future, you always have the impression that you can postpone your actions until tomorrow, that you can start later, and today you can rest. Well, this is wrong. This is not the right state of mind. Sentences in the future begin with tomorrow. They don't have consistency. The best time to act is now.

MY PERFECT LIFE VISUALIZATION EXERCISE
There is an extraordinary power in creative visualization. You might ask, "What is it about?" Creative visualization is a tool that allows you to transform your dreams, your desires, and your ambitions into very clear mental images.

Let's do this exercise together: Think of the big picture of what living your perfect life looks and feels like to you. I want you to meditate on your life vision. Pick a peaceful, relaxing spot where you can be alone. Sit down in a comfortable position and start imagining your ideal life. Mentally put yourself in the position of your best self. Act it. Walk like you're rich. Dress the way you want to look. Talk like you mean it. Smile like you're happy. Imagine the way you want to feel.

You might wonder, "why should I do this?" The reason is to inspire you. To give you ideas of the things you really want for your life. So, go ahead and visualize. Get used to how it feels. When you get used to this image and feeling of who you are, and where you want to be, you will manifest it. You will make it happen!

Who are you becoming? What are you feeling? Where are you going? Just think of your dream life. Take a glimpse of your future with you living your dream life. Block every disbelief and "what ifs" from the mind. Just think freely as if there is no problem or setback in achieving the life you desire. As if you have already acquired the life you desire. As if everything in your life is going the way you want. As if you are in your very own paradise. Think about what you want, not about what you don't want. Permit yourself to dream, be creative. Consider ideas that you never thought possible. Focus on your own wishes, not what others expect of you. What do you see? What does your best life look like? Listen to your intuition and how your body reacts, it should feel expansive.

Below, I have provided some helpful prompts you can use to meditate; to envision your perfect day:
- What do you want to be remembered for?
- What's a great life to you?
- What's a life well-lived to you?
- What will make you satisfied in life?
- What will make you feel free?
- When do you feel your best? (Your flow)
- What have you always wanted to do?

- What matters to you?
- What kind of energy do you want to have?
- How do you want to make others feel?
- What do you enjoy?
- What do you want to be around?
- What do you love to do? (Pick areas that align with your heart, passion, gifts and strengths)
- What matters to you in life? (Not what should matter, but what actually does matter)
- What would you like to have more of in your life?
- Set aside money for a moment; what do you want in your career?
- What are your secret passions and dreams?
- What would bring more joy and happiness into your life?
- What do you want your relationships to be like?
- What qualities would you like to develop?
- What are your values?
- What issues do you care about?
- What are your talents?
- What would you most like to accomplish?
- What legacy would you like to leave behind?

Another method that I recommend is planning backward. Think of all of your dreams and desires as if they have already happened. Reflect on them. Below, there are some prompts to help you start planning backward:

- Who are you?
- What do you do for a living?
- Where do you live?
- Are you with another person, a group of people, or are you by yourself?
- Do you have a partner?
- Do you have kids?

- What kinds of people do you have in your life?
- What kinds of relationships do you have in your life?
- How are you perceived?
- How are you treated?
- What's the last thing that would've had to happen to achieve your best lifestyle?
- What's the most important choice you would've had to make?
- What would you have needed to learn along the way?
- What important actions would you have taken to get there?
- What beliefs would you have needed to change?
- What habits or behaviours would you have had to cultivate?
- What type of support would you have had to enlist?
- How long would it have taken you to realize your best lifestyle?
- What steps or milestones would you have needed to reach along the way?
- How do you feel emotionally, day-to-day?
- What character traits do you possess and express?
- How does your body look and feel?
- Where and how do you live?
- What do you do with your time and life?
- What fun things do you get to enjoy?
- What would you have accomplished already?
- How will you feel about yourself?
- What kinds of people are in your life?
- How do you feel about them?
- What does your ideal day look like?
- Where are you? Where do you live? Think specifics; what city, state, or country, type of community, house or apartment, style, and atmosphere.
- What would you be doing?

- How are you dressed?
- What is your state of mind? Happy or sad? Contented or frustrated?
- What does your physical body look like? How do you feel about that?
- Does your best life make you smile and make your heart sing? If it doesn't, dig deeper, dream bigger.

VISION BOARD

A visualization tool that I recommend is a vision board, especially if you would like something more tangible to look at when you want to visualize. A vision board is a board that you create, filled up with the things you want to acquire in life. Its objectives are similar to a bucket list.

Find images, texts, and other illustrations of places, people and things that inspire you, and put them on your board or on another area you see regularly. You can also include pictures of people you care for, scenes that depict specific memories you love, and anything else you want to invite into your life.

Here are a few ideas of vision board:

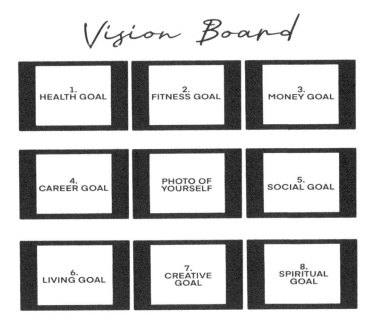

Through these mental images, it is possible to greatly accelerate the process of manifestation. I advise you to create one vision board, at least. It will keep you inspired and help you to keep track of your progress.

Some ideas you can add to your vision board:

Who are you and what are your beliefs?

- Lifestyle
- Goals
- Occupation

What are the things that are important to you?

- Flexible hours
- Fulfilment, in work, life, etc.
- Education
- Spending time with friends and/or family
- Ability to travel
- Freedom
- Hobbies
- Change lives
- Financial stability
- Meditation practice
- Your lifestyle
- Personal and professional development

What do you want to acquire?

- Your dream home
- A sports car
- A new skill
- A business you are passionate about
- An entertaining kitchen
- A personal stylist
- Your ideal body
- A chef

What do you want to learn?

- How to speak French or Italian
- How to dance tango
- How to cook
- How to play an instrument, like the piano, guitar, etc
- How to play a sport

Who do you want to help?

- Families
- Children
- Less fortunate
- Abuse victims
- Animals
- Third-world countries
- Financially, like donating money and fundraisers
- Physically, like volunteering
- Intellectually, like speaking

How do you want to be with your loved ones?

- Keep in touch daily, weekly, monthly
- Keep in touch by phone, email, text
- Live together
- Have experiences together, like traveling, working, adventures

What do you want to achieve?

- Write a book
- Speak on a big stage
- Travel the world
- Hike a mountain
- Go to a retreat
- Attend a seminar
- Go to a concert
- Start a podcast
- Earn a diploma

- Become a millionaire
- Become a billionaire
- Get out of debts
- Save, like $5,000... $20,000... $1 million

After you create your vision board, I want you to meditate on it and believe that you will acquire everything on it. Here's a nice fact: Our brains do not know the difference between when we are practicing a thing, and when it is happening in reality. The brain always thinks that the event is currently happening. It also does not know the difference between when something is currently happening, when you are remembering something that has already happened, and when you are imagining something that you want to happen. The brain thinks everything is happening presently. So whenever you visualize, the brain produces the same chemicals that it does when the event is currently happening. I'm addition, when you visualize, your brain looks for ways to manifest what you're visualizing. This is the reason you should visualize positive things, so positivity manifests into your life. This method is called the law of attraction.

THE LAW OF ATTRACTION
The law of attraction is a universal law that suggests that you become what you focus on. Every single thing that happens in your life begins in your imagination. What you give your energy to has power over you if you allow it. Positive thinking and believing in yourself come back into play. Every moment you believe in yourself, you create momentum for your vision to come true.

The law of attraction is considered to be one of the most popular and potent laws of the universe. Just like gravity, it is always in effect and motion. It suggests that you are consistently in a state of creation. You are constantly shaping your reality at every moment of every day. You are creating your future with every thought, whether your thoughts are intentional or subliminal. Understanding exactly how the law of attraction works is an essential key to your prosperity.

It is a powerful tool that will help you transform your life, and empower you to create an amazing future. Once you understand how connected your world is; anticipate wonders. The law of attraction allows the manifestation of endless possibilities, unbounded abundance, and infinite joy. It is not difficult to practice, and it can change your life inside and out.

Like attracts like

What you put into the universe is brought back to you. The universe gives you exactly what you want. It does not choose which one is better for you, it just responds to whatever energy you make, and it gives you more of the same. You get back precisely what you put out there. If you are feeling energized, excited, enthusiastic, glad, cheerful, thankful, or plentiful, at that point you are conveying positive energy. However, if you are feeling exhausted, on edge, worried, irritated, angry, or dismal, you are conveying negative energy. The law of attraction returns your energy to you.

How to use the law of attraction

STEP 1: Ask the universe for what you want by thinking and focusing on it. Do not think of what you do not want, because you wouldn't want to invite that energy by thinking of it. Try to find answers to these questions:
 How would you feel once you have arrived at your goal? What would you do consistently? Who would you invest time or energy with?

STEP 2: Believe that you will get what you want and take action towards it.

STEP 3: Receive what you want by making yourself a vibrational match for it.

The Law of Attraction is really simple at its core. If you want something, act as if you already have it. Talk as if you already have it. Make room for it to come into your life. By doing so, you manifest your wishes into your life. One popular way to manifest is through affirmations.

AFFIRMATIONS
Affirmations are written or spoken positive statements that when practiced consistently, rewire your thoughts and beliefs. When you repeat them regularly and have confidence in them, you program your brain into believing them. Try looking at affirmations this way: a lot of us do repetitive exercises to improve our physical wellbeing. Well, affirmations are like exercises for our minds and viewpoint. These positive mental reiterations can reprogram your thinking patterns so that, over time, you start to think and act them involuntarily.

Affirmations are techniques that allow you to design for the future in which you will state in the present tense the events that you hope will happen in the future, but speaking of them as if they were already accomplished. Affirmations are like incantations.

Why should you make affirmations? Well, that is a valid question. What if I tell you that affirmations work because they can program your psyche into accessing and accepting the repeated statements and concepts? Add it to the law of attraction, and you will manifest your affirmations.

Affirmations are good because they:

- It motivates you to act. Furthermore, when you set actions to your goals, affirmations further increase your desire to continue your actions.
- It directs your focus to your goals. Goal achievement is helped by persistently keeping your mind centred on the goal.
- It switches your negative thought patterns into positive ones.
- It influences your subconscious mind to adopt new beliefs.
- It assists you with feeling positive about yourself and lifts your self-assurance.

Affirmations mostly prove to be useful when you need to induce a positive state, for
example:

- Raise your confidence before presentations or important meetings.
- Control negative feelings, for example, disappointment, outrage, or restlessness.
- Improve your self-esteem.
- Finish projects you have begun.
- Improve your productivity.
- Conquer a negative behaviour pattern.

How do you create affirmations to fit your needs?
1. Consider the aspects of your life that you want to change. For example, you might wish that you had more patience, or more profound relationships with your friends and colleagues, or even a more productive workday. List the

43

areas that you would like to work on. Make sure they are compatible with your core values/principles and the things that generally matter to you so that you will feel genuinely persuaded to accomplish them.

2. Be certain that your affirmation is credible and attainable. Base it on a realistic evaluation of the facts. For example, pretend that you are dissatisfied with the degree of job pay that you are getting presently. You could utilize affirmations to increase your confidence to request a raise. Keep it practical. All things considered, affirmations are not enchantment spells; if you cannot trust them, it is unlikely that they will affect your life.

3. Transform negativity into positivity. If you are battling with negative self-talk, note down the persistent thoughts or convictions that are disturbing you. After that, pick an affirmation that is something contrary to that thought or conviction.

4. State your affirmation in the present tense. Write and speak your affirmation as though it is already occurring. This encourages you to believe that the statement is true at the present time. For example, "I am solid, steady, and all-around practiced, and I can give an incredible presentation" would be an ideal affirmation to utilize if you feel anxious about talking before a gathering.

5. Say it with emotional attachment. Affirmations are increasingly powerful when they convey passionate weight. You have to need this change to happen, so every affirmation that you decide to repeat ought to be an expression that is important to you. For instance, if you are stressed over a

project that you have been assigned to do, you could say to yourself, "I am truly eager to take on new tasks."

A more simple system:
To use affirmations, first, analyze the thoughts or behaviour patterns that you would like to change in your life. Next, concoct positive, trustworthy, and attainable affirmation statements that are something contrary to these thoughts. Finally, rehearse your affirmations multiple times each day, particularly when you end up slipping into negative self-talk or participate in negative conduct.

Checklist for making affirmations:
- It has to be convincing to you
- It has to be within your control
- It has to be in present terms
- It must be positively worded
- It must cause you to feel good
- You have to feel it
- You have to repeat it consistently

When people make affirmations, they say things like:
- I am creating what I want
- I am getting what I want
- I am empowered
- I am blessed
- I am getting everything I came for
- My problems are ending
- Good things are happening to me
- My dreams have come true
- I am a new and thriving person
- My life is always improving
- The universe is giving me all that I desire

- Everything that I need to create my dream life is within me
- My work is perceived positively by my boss and associates
- My team members respect and value my opinion
- I am successful
- I am straightforward in my life and my work
- I always complete assignments and activities on schedule
- I am appreciative of the life I have
- I enjoy working with my team
- I bring an uplifting disposition to work every day
- I am fantastic at what I do
- I am liberal
- I am happy
- I am the innovator in my organization

You can use the affirmations below to help you manifest your best lifestyle:

- My dream success flows towards me like a river
- I am a natural magnet of everything that I wish to achieve
- I am where I want to be
- Despite the odds, my dreams are flowing towards me
- My dream of becoming a millionaire has come to live
- I am attracting the right situations that will help me reach my best lifestyle
- Everything is happening at the right time and in the right place to help me achieve my best lifestyle
- Opportunities appear to me naturally and help me get closer to my best lifestyle
- I am living my best lifestyle
- My best lifestyle is getting closer to me with each passing day

My Life Vision

- I shall achieve my goals with the help of the universe
- Success is like skin to me
- The universe is acting following my best lifestyle
- Achievement is a natural outcome of everything that I do
- I am a magnet to a positive result
- Everything that happens is for my good
- Success flows in my direction
- I am appreciated for everything that I have achieved
- I always appreciate myself for my hard work
- I always make time to appreciate myself for all the hard work I put in to achieve my best lifestyle
- I set examples for others by achieving my best lifestyle
- With each passing day, I become better at my work
- I have become a better human in the journey of achieving my best lifestyle
- Every day I plan to achieve better and more in my life
- I am always thankful for the satisfaction I feel after I achieve my best lifestyle
- The universe always lays out a helping hand for me
- I manifest everything that I want to manifest
- I manifest one miracle after the other
- The way I achieve my best lifestyle is considered a miracle by many
- I have achieved financial freedom
- My dreams and goals are endless
- The universe is full of infinite possibilities and I am manifesting all of them
- I am going to achieve more than I have imagined
- My imagination has no limit and so does my best lifestyle
- I have ample time to achieve everything that I want
- I create time from my busy schedule for everything that is important to me

47

- I agree that fear implies that I am on the right track to achieving my best lifestyle
- I am stuck on my goals and I shall not stop before I achieve all of them
- I have the required strength to keep moving forward towards my best lifestyle
- I am surrounded by love that keeps me moving towards my best lifestyle
- Money keeps coming my way
- I am always happy and that keeps me going towards my best lifestyle

The trick is to believe everything that you say. This way, your mind, body, and spirit will be open to receiving all of the things that you desire from the universe. If you repeat something enough times, it can become your reality.

Keep making affirmations until you finally achieve all your goals. Affirmations are more effective when paired with other positive thinking and goal-setting techniques. We will discuss highly reflective goal-setting methods later in this book.
"Everything happens twice; first in mind and then in reality." - Robin Sharma

THE MIRRORING VISUALIZATION TECHNIQUE
I want to introduce you to this method of visualization. In this method, you simply model after your role model(s). Think of a person you want to be like, and ask yourself what you like about them.

Think of people you've seen and admired. People you want to be like. Which people are living your dream lifestyle? What do you like about them? What traits of theirs do you want to embody? What things did they own that you would also like to own? What do they do that makes you admire them? Think of people that inspire you and find out what they did to get there.

Take into consideration things like these. Did they:
- Learn a specific skill?
- Have a certain degree?
- Have certain habits?
- Have certain traits?
- Have a certain mindset?
- What do they have in common?
- What pattern do you notice?
- What are they consistent about?
- What advice did they give?

All you have to do is copy their approaches to become like them. Practice your best lifestyle until you start living it.

CHAPTER FOUR

MY LIFE DESIGN

N ow that you have completed the visualization exercise, you should have ideas about the kind of life you want to live. You are ready to design your life to your taste.

After designing your life, you will move to the next group of activities, which I call "amazing goal-setting." In this section, you will learn how to set amazing goals, just as the name suggests.

The "amazing goal-setting" section is divided into four main categories:

Brainstorm: You will decide and set goals for what you want to accomplish, for each area of your life.

Simplify: You will add up your goals into umbrella goals.

Prioritize: You will put your goals on a timeline and delegate them as long, medium and short-term goals.

Action Plan: You will decide which goal(s) to begin with. You will add the goals to your daily schedule and create habits to help accomplish your goals.

Before you start setting goals, you will design your life.

WHAT IS YOUR LIFE DESIGN?

Designing one's life is a conscious adjustment of fate, where unhealthy programs are removed from the structure, and new ones that contribute to happiness are implanted. Is it possible to design your own life? Of course. You can build a strong foundation from education, build walls from strong relationships, and floors from reliable work. In fact, no matter which part of your life path you are currently at, it is possible to organize it, and bring it into a coherent structure. To do this, you need to look back and carefully study the path that you have already travelled. This path will very clearly demonstrate your life scenario, identify all repetitive sequences, show where you step on the same rake over and over again, and adjust as needed to create a more cohesive life.

Designing your life means that you are leaving the game, you are leaving the play, you're leaving the life scenario of which you were living, and becoming something else. You can change your role in life, because you are not only the actor, but also the director, the C.E.O, and any other ownership role you wish to take on for your life. You don't have to play victim or end up in a tragedy at the end, you can decide to change your own story. You have the right to create beautiful endings with your life. You can switch roles in the play that is your life. The main thing is to realize that you are in control of your life. At this very moment, you are absolutely free; you can go and do whatever you want with your life. It's time to take the pen from your parents, as well as other important people from your childhood and your life in general, and write for yourself your very best lifestyle.

WHY YOU NEED TO DESIGN YOUR LIFE

Some of your most unhealthy programs were put into you during childhood, at an age when you were not able to analyze what you were told and what was done to you. At a tender age, you were more likely to perceive your interferences as the ultimate truth. For example, if a mother often tells her child that he/she is bad, that child can accept that attitude for a long time, maybe even for the rest of their life. If the kid is told that nothing good will come from him/her, and believes it, the kid can grow up and not bother striving for greatness.

This is a reason why the conscious design of one's life is so important because negative life scenarios are dangerous and destroy life. Look at this example. If a little girl observes the rude behaviour of her father towards her mother, in adulthood, it can become the norm for her. Growing up, she is more likely to repeat that scenario. She's also more likely to be attracted to rude men who resemble her father, which means that rudeness will be present in her family life. Even though she might suffer from this, she might think it's logical, as this is a familiar situation to her. But if suddenly she meets a gentleman who isn't rude, then her life scenario will change. On the one hand, she might think that she is lucky to have met him, and on the other, she might consider the man to be weak.

In addition to the scripts laid down in childhood, life events that occur throughout life can greatly affect your life path. These are unexpected turning points in fate, which hit your human psyche and affected your attitude towards life. Unhappy love, death of a loved one, fires, floods, forced relocation - are examples of life events that might have left a tough imprint. After such shocks, it is very important to design your future life. After all, everyone comes out of life's cataclysms in different ways: some people end up so tragic that they sink to the bottom and never emerge from there, living out the rest of their lives cursing fate. While others pull themselves together, go forward step by step, overcome difficulties and as a result, their life paths become success stories.

I understand that it might seem scary to take full responsibility of your life all by yourself, to start designing your own life. It is much easier to blame everyone and everything for your unhappy fate. It's simpler, but NOT more effective. Yes! Life scenarios and fateful events put pressure on us, they are like a rut into which we have been driven and it might seem convenient to move in accordance with them. If you are not satisfied with your current situation, then you need to get out of the rut, and maybe even crawl off-road, but with the awareness of personal choice. That's when you need to analyze and repurpose your life.

HOW TO DESIGN YOUR LIFE
You should take a closer look at your life. Examine it closely. That's what this next activity is about. This activity is about rating your life categories. The goal of this activity is to give you a visual evaluation of your life because most people learn more effectively with visualization. This exercise will help you evaluate your current situations in different areas of your life, and identify areas that are and are not being fulfilled to the level of your satisfaction.

To start working on this activity, I would highly advise you to start keeping a journal.

JOURNALING
Journals help you monitor and track your progress in life. They also serve as referral guides or archives, for every time you need to remember what you need to do and how to do it, by referring back to your action plan to carry out your projects and plans.

An alternative to journaling is making to-do lists. Similarly, the combination of various to-do lists in one single book can also form a journal. To be able to keep your to-do lists all in one place, you can use daily planners, whiteboards or vision boards, or even planning applications if you prefer a digital route. An alternative to the hybrid system is called bullet journaling. Regardless of the planning system of your choice, one highly important thing is to make sure you keep your system somewhere visible and easily accessible to you at all times.

Your to-do list will be filled with goals to help you achieve the life you desire. Hence, it is crucial that you get a full assessment of what your life goals are before you start designing your life.

LIFE CATEGORIES
I have come up with 10 key areas that make up our lives, however, you can change the category titles to sections that suit you better. I believe there are 10 main areas in life:
1. Spirituality
2. Personal Development
3. Family and Friends
4. Career
5. Finances
6. Personal Environment
7. Health and Fitness
8. Romance and Significant Other
9. Fun and Recreation
10. Giving/Contribution

In your journal or other writing tool, observe and rate each of the areas of your life based on your current level of satisfaction with them. Rate them from 1 to 10, with 1 being the lowest and 10 being the highest. Write down your ratings of how you currently feel about each area. To give you an idea, please refer to the figure below:

Life Assessment

(MY CURRENT LEVEL OF SATISFACTION)

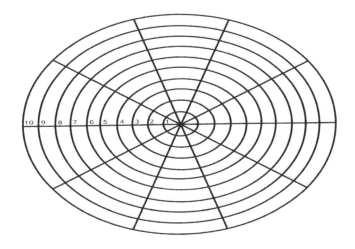

BRAINSTORM

In this section, you should think of ideas for your best lifestyle. Assess your entire life and decide what exactly you want for each given area.

Assess each area of your life and ask these six questions:

1. What is my premise for this area? (Your beliefs and purpose about the area)

2. What do I want for this area?

3. Why do I want that for this area?

4. What do I need to do to be fully satisfied with this area?

5. What actions do I need to begin or increase to support my vision for this area?

6. What actions do I need to stop or reduce to support my vision for this area?

55

After that exercise, you should have a clearer plan for your best lifestyle. Take note of your answers in your writing tool. These answers should have a major influence on the life goals you will set for your best lifestyle.

Below you can find more questions to take into consideration as you set your life goals.

- Aesthetic: Would you like to get familiar with an instrument? Partake in a play? See the Mona Lisa? How might you get that going?
- Disposition: Is any piece of your attitude keeping you down? Are there specific practices or habits that are upsetting to you and that you might want to change? Do you need anyone to help you with these changes?
- Vocation: What level would you like to reach in your profession? What amount of instruction will you need? Is your activity fulfilling? Does it mirror your qualities? Do you have a chance to grow?
- Training: Is there any information you need to secure specifically? What data and aptitudes will you have to accomplish? What are your objectives?
- Family/Companions: Would you like to be a parent? Will you hold back on having kids until you have a great job? Where do you imagine your family living? On the off chance that you now have children, is there something explicit you might want to accomplish for/with them? Do you have/need a nearby friend available for assistance? Do you invest enough energy in your relationship with your loved ones? Do you value the relationship you have with one another?
- Cash and Funds: What salary would you like to be earning and at what phase of your life? Would you like to get raises, retirement, and 401ks? How might you achieve that? Do you make enough? Do you have

sufficient spare time? Are you getting ready for a monetary opportunity?

- Physical: Are there any athletic objectives you need to accomplish? How would you like to keep up great health into mature age? What steps would you say you are going to take to accomplish this?

"If you want to live a happy life, tie it to a goal, not to people or things." -Albert Einstein

LIFE GOALS

Life goals are what you need to accomplish in your lifetime to feel the fulfilment and satisfaction driven from them. They are significantly more important than what you have to achieve just to survive. They are completely different from your regular everyday schedules. They come from within you and encourage you to pursue your desires as time goes on. Life goals will help you focus on the kind of life you want to live, aligning with your values and fulfilling your true calling.

At the most simple level, a life goal is a desire, objective, or outcome you wish to achieve for your life. However, because goals are personal desires, they can take a wide range of structures. They provide you a feeling of guidance and make you more responsible as you make progress towards joy and prosperity for your most ideal life.

Did you know, when you write down your goals, you are 50% more likely to accomplish them than when you do not? It is important, isn't it?

Why are life goals important?

Everyone has dreams. During your lifetime, you might have realized what fulfils you, what you would love to try, and certain things you may have ambiguous thoughts about, even including how you would go about it. In any case, defining clear goals can be valuable in a few different ways. Here are a couple:

1. Defining goals determine and clarify your practices. The act of defining objectives and the idea you put into creating them guides your focus towards the why, how, and what of your yearnings.

2. Goals help you accept constructive criticism. If or when you know where you want to be, you can assess where you are now, and essentially, you can chart your progress. This feedback helps you adjust your behavior accordingly. By allowing for feedback, goals let you align or realign your behavior, keeping you on track with your eyes on the prize.

3. Goals boost happiness. When your goals are based on your values, they are meaningful. Meaning, purpose, and striving for something bigger is a key element of happiness. In other words, life goals represent something besides the daily grind. They allow you to pursue authentic aims of your choosing and enjoy feelings of achievement when you get there. That said, just striving to be the very best can sometimes lead to happiness in itself.

4. Goals urge you to utilize your strengths or qualities. When you consider what matters the most to you, you can get more attuned with your inner strengths as well as your passions. Charting a course for yourself is one thing, but using your strengths to get there comes with a whole set of other benefits. Studies show that knowing and leveraging your strengths can increase your confidence, boost your

engagement, and even promote feelings of good health and life satisfaction.

5. Goals give you something which you can look forward to, which builds hope. You can plan whatever you enjoy- a party, a trip, a home improvement project, personal journey, etc. The act of planning is therapeutic, and you'll have something to keep you motivated moving forward.

Goal setting can also:
- Spotlight your sights on something you need to achieve
- Manage the why, when, and how of your life
- Transform your fantasies and dreams into the real world
- Allow you to organize the point-by-point steps expected to arrive at your desires
- Assist breaks, by bringing down overpowering bigger undertakings into littler sensible assignments
- Encourage better time-management
- Prompt a feeling of achievement and self-satisfaction

"Our goals can only be reached through a vehicle of a plan, in which we must fervently believe, and upon which we must vigorously act. There is no other route to success." -Pablo Picasso

What motivates a goal?
Now that I've told you why life goals are valuable, let's move on to understand the different types of life goal motivators.

Life goals are subjective. They are different for each individual, based on each individual's values and priorities. There are two motivators of life goals, and their classifications depend on your reason for wanting them. Goals are either intrinsically or extrinsically motivated. Intrinsic goals are goals that are lined up with your requirements as a person, mirroring your self-awareness and building more satisfying connections. On the other hand, extrinsic goals are more socially characterized.

In other words, intrinsic life goals are based on the motivation that comes from your inner world, whereas extrinsic life goals are formed to gain societal acceptance. Intrinsic life goals are often based on inward pursuits to fulfil the necessities that come from being a human.

Some examples of intrinsic life goals might include:
- Having a passionate marriage or confiding in a relationship with your better half Finding and keeping a solid work-life balance, with time for loved ones
- Living with honesty, being straightforward and open with others
- Moving others through your convictions and activities
- Being a confidant so that others can go to you
- Turning into a specialist in your field and helping other people

Since intrinsic goals come from your needs as a human, Maslow's hierarchy of needs is a good source of intrinsic goals. Abraham Maslow, a former American Psychologist, proposed a popular framework called "A theory of Human Motivation," which is displayed in the diagram below:

Intrinsic self-actualization goals could involve:

Thinking of another development that mirrors your innovative capacities

Being an effective business visionary and maintaining your own business

Making your very own image for your work

Graduating with a Master's degree or Ph.D.

Learning another language

Gaining and perfecting a new expertise

Unlike intrinsic, extrinsic life goals are usually based on wants instead of needs. However, unlike the perception, they are not always material. Also, these goals require less self-reflection when setting.

Some examples of extrinsic life goals might include:

Purchasing the most recent or highest-grade luxury vehicle

Gaining tycoon status

61

Getting promoted or being in an executive position at your workplace
Featuring in a film
Having a workshop/studio
Visiting a European country

Intrinsic goals are favoured more than extrinsic goals because they are more meaningful. However, regardless of whether your goal is intrinsically or extrinsically motivated, it is important to always have good intentions. Having the 'right' purpose behind goal interest, regardless of the goal itself, has been found to add to your prosperity.

A life without goals

A life without goals is a life that is going nowhere, or running a race with no endpoint. While there are genuine advantages to goal-setting, how bad is it to not set any goal? Setting goals creates an environment that allows more positivity and less negativity. It also creates an environment of excellence and satisfaction in one's capabilities.

Good thing that you are reading this book, right? Now that you know all about life goals, it is time to design your ideal lifestyle. Once you complete this task, you will set more specific goals that will help bring your big picture into your reality.

How to choose life goals

How should you decide your life goals? When you look around, you will be able to find inspirations all around you, but because the meaning needs to be intrinsic, your reason should be unique. To discover where your interests and values lie, I will provide you with a little exercise. Ask yourself the questions below:

1. What precisely do you want? You can take a self-reflection assessment to discover your inner desires.

2. Why do you want them? What do you believe they will do for you? Make sure you want them for the right reasons.

3. Make sure these goals are your personal desires for yourself and not someone else's goals for you. You are less likely to follow through on something that you do not truly want.

Now let's decide on what would make you feel fulfilled. You can answer these questions on a writing tool, e.g. your journal:

1. What were your childhood dreams?

2. If you could be anybody, who would you be?

3. What did you once want, stopped wanting, or could not go through with, but it still lingers in your mind? Decide if you still want it.

4. What do you not want? If you do not know what exactly you want, decide what you do not want and choose the opposite of it.

5. What's your life's purpose?

It all came full circle now, didn't it? Another convenient way of creating your list of life goals is to brainstorm ideas in each of the following categories:
- Who you want to BE
- What you want to DO
- What you want to LEARN

- What you want to HAVE
- What you want to GIVE

SMART GOALS

As you set goals for each area of your life, I would like to teach you how to set goals like a professional by using the SMART goal-setting method. This name is an acronym for Specific, Measurable, Attainable, Relevant, and Timely goals. Let me explain this method more in-depth.

Specific: Well defined, clear, and precise. Your goal needs to be clear and well-defined by what you need to accomplish.

To make sure your goal is specific, you can ask yourself:
- Who: Who is engaged with this goal?
- What: What do I want to achieve?
- Where: Where is this goal going to be accomplished?
- When: When would I like to achieve this goal?
- Why: For what reason would I like to achieve this goal?
- How: How will I find a way to accomplish this objective?

For instance, a life goal could be "I want to graduate from a college." A more specific goal is "I want to graduate from Prestige University, with a bachelor's degree in Human Happiness."

Questions to identify specific goals: Is your goal(s) specific enough? Is it something that could be easily identified when you have arrived at it? If not, how could you make it more specific?

Measurable: Specific benchmarks that measure progress towards completion. You need to be able to track the progress of your goal, as well as know when your goal has been accomplished. If there are no standards, you will not be able to determine your progress to see if you are on target to arrive at your goal.

To make sure your goal is measurable, you can ask yourself:
- How many/much?
- How would I know whether I have arrived at my goal?
- How do I gauge my progress?

For instance, building on a measurable part of the specific goal above: "I want to graduate from Prestige University with a bachelor's degree in Human Happiness in the year 2024."

Questions to recognize measurable goals: Is your goal(s) measurable? Would you be able to tell me when you have arrived at it? Is there a clear standard to find out? If not, how could you make it more measurable?

Attainable/Actionable: Attainable, reasonable, and reasonable. You have to trust that you can achieve your goal. The goal has an activity that aligns with your big picture. The achievability of the goal might cause you to feel challenged, however, defined well enough that you can finish it.

To make sure your goal is attainable, you can ask yourself:
- Do I have the assets and capabilities to accomplish the goal? If not, what am I missing?
- Have others successfully finished this goal previously?

Questions to distinguish achievable goals: Is your goal(s) achievable? Is it something that you have thought of and understand how it is, truth be told, possible, and able to be accomplished? If not, how might you alter your goal and/or time desires to make it attainable?

Relevant: Realistic, reasonable to your interests, and significant to you. Your goal has to be important to you and will assist you in achieving our greater vision. It must be sensible in that given the accessible resources and time; you can finish the goal.

To make sure your goal is relevant, you can ask yourself:
- Is my goal reasonable and attainable?
- Is my goal reachable given the time and resources?
- Can I commit myself to achieve the goal?

Questions to distinguish realistic goals:
Is your goal(s) realistic? If it is big and challenging, that is great, but is it something that you are:
1. Physically and mentally equipped to perform?
2. Prepared for it? And
3. Able to commit to?

If not, is there another approach to arrive at your goal, another similar goal, or something you can do to make this one within reach?

Timely: has a stipulated time frame, has a starting and ending date. Your goal needs to have a specific time frame. Your time frames are your start date, finish date, period, timeline, and so forth. If the goal does not have a deadline, there will be less desire and motivation to achieve the objective.

To make sure your goal is timely, you can ask yourself:
- Does my goal have a deadline?

- By when would I like to achieve my goal?

For instance, expanding on the previous example: I will complete my general education and prerequisites for a Human Happiness degree at Success College by Spring 2022, transfer to Prestige University in Fall 2022 and graduate with a Bachelor's of Arts Degree in Human Happiness, in 2024.

Questions to recognize timely goals: Does your goal(s) have time? Have you marked the calendar or set the duration? Do you have a sense of urgency for the next step? If not, is there something else you need to do to be able to put your goal on a timeline and begin taking the necessary actions?

Here are some prompts to help you assess if your goals fall into this framework:
Is the goal achievable?
Can I accomplish my goal within the time I have set?
Does achieving this goal depend only on me and not on conditions outside of me?
Do I believe I can achieve this goal?
Are my skills and abilities equal to this goal?
Will I know when I have reached my goal?
Have I set my goal in specific terms?
Do I want to do what it takes to reach my goal?
Is the goal one that interests me?
Is the goal presented with an alternative?
Have I made a firm decision?
Do I have an alternative if I cannot reach my goal?
Do I have a support system?
Have I set up a timeline towards my goal?
Do I have a reward system in place?
Is the goal of value to me?

Is the goal compatible with my values?
Does my goal have longevity?
Do I need to consider more education?

Below you can find a chart to help you assess your goals in the SMART framework.

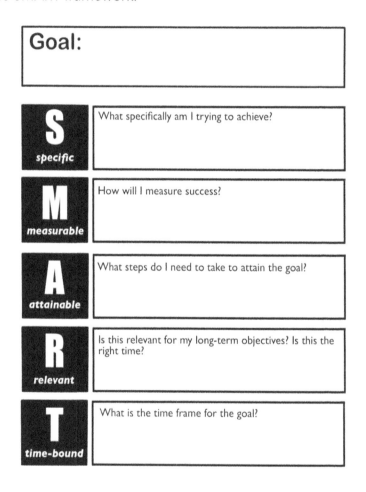

Goal:

S specific	What specifically am I trying to achieve?
M measurable	How will I measure success?
A attainable	What steps do I need to take to attain the goal?
R relevant	Is this relevant for my long-term objectives? Is this the right time?
T time-bound	What is the time frame for the goal?

Let's look at these examples of a SMART goals:

EXAMPLE 1: "I want to run a marathon on July 19

Action: I want to run
Specific, Measurable, Relevant: a marathon
Time: on July 1

EXAMPLE 2: "I want to start learning Spanish next week."
Specific, Measurable, Relevant, and Attainable/Action: I want to start learning Spanish
Time: next week.

One last step that I would like to add to this goal-setting process is "outcomes." Is your goal composed based on the results you desire and not just the "task" you want to be achieved? What are the outcomes you are searching for? Do you have to fix how you have worded your goals to be centred on the result?

Now that we have brainstormed your goals, we can move on to other "amazing goal- setting" steps.

SIMPLIFY
You need to simplify the goals you had just set. Look at your list of goals and group items that are similar or that can be combined into one larger goal. Goals that are similar in terms of procedures and results can be grouped together to form only one goal. This process of simplifying your goals makes it easier for you to manage your goals.

The rest of the "amazing goal-setting" techniques continue in the next chapter.

MY LIFE BLUEPRINT

Having goals in life can help you motivate yourself and work towards them. In this process, it is essential to have a life blueprint. You have taken a very good step in the previous chapter by setting your life goals. Now that you have set your life goals, the next action for you to take is to create a plan towards achieving them. These plans will make your life goals a reality. To be able to achieve this, you will need a step-by-step action plan to be in place. This action plan is the blueprint for achieving your goals; which is simply "My Life Blueprint."

Getting what you want is in your hand. But, let's start at the beginning; you need to know the meaning of your life blueprint and why you must develop yours. Also, creating a life blueprint is a huge job. This is not something that can be done in an hour, in fact, it can take several weeks. I will also help you to achieve that in this chapter.

WHAT IS YOUR LIFE BLUEPRINT?
Your life blueprint is a document that contains your vital objectives and the actions that you plan to take to achieve them. These vital goals can be of several types:
• Professionals
• Personal
• Economical
• Learning
• Spiritual
• Family

There are many areas of your life in which you can design a blueprint, so it is important to analyze each of them. The objectives can be short-term, medium-term or long-term. To achieve a long-term goal (for example, working on something that you are passionate about), you need to set medium and short-term goals (acquire new skills, search for companies, do interviews, etc.). That is, you must think about the actions that will lead you to your final goal. Another fundamental aspect is to review carrying out the actions that you have proposed according to a period of time. Continuing with the previous example, if you want to change jobs and need the training to have new skills, you can consider the maximum term to take a course and check if you have met that goal. In this sense, you must be realistic and set goals that are possible even if they pose a challenge.

THE IMPORTANCE OF LIFE BLUEPRINT
Between dream, reality, and the realization of your needs, there is an art of giving yourself a concrete and realistic plan, an art of creating it, and an art of making it happen. This is the art of thinking, acting, and becoming the architect and artist of your life.

Building a project is a bit like leaping into a void, towards change, from the impossible to the possible, from the abstract to the concrete. It is the leap to cross the line that marks the boundary between dream and reality.

The following are the importance of having a life blueprint:
1. It helps to train your foresight
For many, when they hear the word "blueprint", they usually think of precise and meticulous planning, with a structured plan for the execution of a job. The expression "plans for the future" instead refers to the dimension of dreams and

intentions. Having goals without putting up a realistic plan to achieve them is more like daydreaming about your desires for years to come. By creating a life blueprint to achieve your goals, you train and develop your foresight, you leave the short and medium-term and you stretch your gaze beyond the visible horizon.

2. It enables you to make decisions in the present

Even if the plans for the future are only a rough idea at the moment, by virtue of that idea you can make decisions that orient your present towards that desire. For example, if you want to be a lawyer, you will rather choose law in the university rather than mathematics. Of course, as you progress through the years, you may want to change your mind due to your present experiences and circumstances but the plans (the blueprint) that you have designed for your life will guide your decision-making and keep you head-on to your future.

3. Reinforce optimism

I am not talking about the vulgar optimism based on the idea that "somehow things will settle down" but the concrete possibility of realizing your goals; this time understood in a literal sense, using the experience and wisdom acquired. If you build on your efforts today, you will be able to visualize the results of those efforts in the future.

4. Feed hope

One of the reasons why it is important to make plans for the future at this time is to nurture the hope that your current situation will change. Hope is not fully nourished by saying "everything will be fine" but by working hard every day to make your vision come true. If you are unable to plan for the future, your present will become too cumbersome and prevent you from looking at what lies beyond the horizon of the present moment.

Finally, I want to give you a task that only you can do. Begin by imagining that you wake up one morning and find yourself face to face with an extraordinary and successful being who surpasses you in all aspects; however, the most amazing thing is that he has the same face. By detailing it, you discover that it is a true and exact copy of you; but in an improved version. When you talk to him, he reminds you that there are great potentials within you that you are not fully utilizing and with which you can be leveraged to reach higher levels of development. Hence, your job is to start working today to transform yourself into that privileged being that you can become. Keep in mind that no matter how old you are, there is always time to do it.

The easiest way to accomplish this task is to take control of your existence. This is only achieved by writing and executing your life plan. I guarantee that in no time you will become the character you want and can become. That will be your greatest reward and, above all, your greatest pride!

Since you have set your life goals, you need to decide when you want to accomplish your goals. The next step is to prioritize your goals.

PRIORITIZE
The truth is that not all goals are created equal, some goals will be more important to you than others. You can't compare buying your dream home to buying a couple of new clothes.

Prioritize the more important goals first, then plan the rest for later. When choosing which goals to work on, it says best to work with the law of 3. This law states that you decide which top three goals are the most important to you and focus on them the most. The purpose of doing this is to help you focus on your more important goals. Prioritizing your goals might cause you to eliminate less important goals. Who knows? Life is pretty unpredictable.

One way of seeing which goals are more important is by ranking them on a scale. As long as you systematically apply the same ranking system to all of the goals that you are assessing, the most important ones should stand out. An alternative to this system would be categorizing your goals first and then ranking them within their categories. You might prefer certain categories because they fall more in line with your core values. This is a good idea if you want to ensure maximum happiness.

Prioritizing isn't only about deciding which goals are or aren't important, but also deciding which goals should come before the other. For example, some goals will take 5 years to accomplish, while some others will take 5 days to accomplish. Aiming for the 5-day goal first doesn't mean that the 5-year goal is less important to you. It's just logical that you would pursue it first before it's no longer available.

Speaking of goals that might no longer be available, there's something interesting that happens in life. You might come across opportunities that you didn't plan for but now have access to. These opportunities might be good for your progress in life. You should add them to your goals and prioritize them accordingly. Life brings good surprises like these.

You can prioritize your goals by creating a timeline. A timeline is a graphic representation of the passage of time as a line. You can mark your timeline in years, months and days. You can mark it by 5 years, example 5, 10, 15, 20, etc. Mark your timeline however you want. You can also have multiple timelines.

A good way of creating a timeline is by setting short-, medium-, and long-term goals.

SHORT TERM, MEDIUM-TERM, AND LONG-TERM GOALS
Achieving goals largely depends on their correct setting, which often helps to translate all your dreams and desires into clear goals that are pleasant and easy to achieve. In addition, know that only you will be responsible for the formation of the goal and for its achievement, and you will not be able to shift the blame onto other people's shoulders. And for you to be sure that you are moving in the right direction, formulate your goals correctly and write them down in your journal. The goal which is only in our head is just a dream that is not taken seriously. The formulation of the goal helps to find the means and strength for its implementation, and the process of forming the goal itself includes the active work of the brain and subconsciousness and gives a person confidence in the final result.

Although at first glance it seems that the formation of goals is not a particularly difficult task, and this is available to everyone, this is not entirely true, because truly successful people, setting goals, manage not only to correctly distribute their efforts but also to evaluate their life as a whole, seeing the prospects and ways to achieve them. This global view helps to increase your motivation and achieve success in life.

Essentially, there are three types of goals:

1.   Short term goals
2.   Medium term goals
3.   Long term goals

1. Short-Term Goals: Goals for 1 year or less.

The short-term goals are "short" for a purpose. They bridge the gap between where you are right now and where you want to be. These goals are to be accomplished within a short time frame not more than a year.

Why are short-term goals important?

- They let you create effective strategies
- They provide quick feedback
- They help kill procrastination
- They keep your focus

Some examples of short-term goals:

- Exercise 4 days a week
- Pay off a few small debts
- Save a specific amount of money for an emergency fund
- Save money for a trip coming soon
- Learn a new hobby
- Lose 20 lbs.
- Take a class
- Go on monthly dates with your special someone
- Buy a DSLR camera
- Take a trip

2. Medium Term Goals: Goals for 3 to 5 years.

A medium-term goal is one that takes a bit longer. Your medium-term goals will often be set as a result of achieving short-term targets; they are often driven by the achievement of short- term goals. They aid in future long-term goals.

Some examples of medium-term goals:
- Finish a bachelor's or master's degree program Move to a new city
- Change careers
- Purchase a house
- Pay off all debts (probably not including a mortgage)
- Start a family

3. Long-Term Goals: Goals for 10 years and above.
Long-term goals can be achieved by using a series of short and medium -term goals as stepping stones along the way to the endpoint. Breaking down your longer-term targets into a series of smaller (and thus more achievable) steps is a great way to ensure your ultimate success.

Some examples of long-term goals:
- Retire early
- Pay off mortgage
- Pay for children to go to college
- Be able to purchase a vacation home
- Plan for children's weddings

Planning any more than 10 years is notoriously tricky (at least without a crystal ball or a time machine) because life is unpredictable, but that's not to say you can't set such long term goals, especially in terms of an exit plan for example. You just need to be prepared to continually adapt and adjust to take account of changing situations. You must always keep in mind that several short-term goals add together to achieve a medium-term goal, and eventually your long-term bigger goal. It will help you to set your focus and see where you are heading, identify your next steps to take, and check your progress if you are in the direction.

"If the plan doesn't work, change the plan but never change the goal." – Unknown

Now, let's circle back to your goals. Assess your goals for each area of your life, and decide when exactly you want to accomplish them. Each of your goals will fit into one of the three categories: short term, medium term, or long-term goals. After putting your goals in their proper categories, you'll know which goals to begin with sooner than the others. Start by dechunking your life goals.

Your long-term goals are gotten from your life goals. They are those goals that you set to achieve your ultimate life.

Each of your long-term goals are broken down into a series of medium-term goals, which are in turn broken down into a series of short-term goals. For example, if you want to become a doctor as your long-term goal, your medium-term goal can be to graduate with a bachelor's degree. After graduating with a bachelor's degree, your next medium-term goal would be to acquire the next degree. Then your next medium-term goal would be to complete residency, and so on. You keep setting medium term goals for your long-term goal until you achieve your long-term goal. In this case, you keep setting medium term goals until you become a doctor.

Each of your medium-term goals are further broken down into smaller goals called short term goals. For example, if your medium-term goal is to earn a bachelor's degree, your short-term goals would be passing each course until you acquire the degree.

ACTION PLAN

After choosing long, medium-, and short-term goals, the next step is to create an action plan or execution so you can start working on your goals immediately.

Be careful not to wait for the perfect time. Find a good, calm time to work on your goals, but keep in mind that the best time to start your goals isn't simply achievable because the best time is now. Look for things you can begin doing immediately. Either use a planner, an agenda, or even the journal, you have to put your plans into schedules so you can start working on them. You can start living your best lifestyle today!

As a general rule of thumb, you should actively focus on your short-term plans because they are the goals that you want to accomplish the soonest. The sooner you want to achieve the goal, the sooner you should start working on it. Some goals can be worked on passively. Some goals need preparation, months, and even years, before achieving them. For example, if you want to buy a house in 5 years, you can start saving your money for the house now or start researching the type of house you want. Here's another example, if your long-term goal is to become a successful entrepreneur, a goal you can start with today would be selecting the perfect business venture you want to start. Break down your goals into smaller chunks. Break down your long-term plans into yearly plans. Break down your yearly plans into monthly plans. Break down your monthly plans into weekly plans. Break down your weekly plans into daily plans. Break down your daily plans into single tasks. Eventually, you will accomplish each task, step by step, until you reach your final goal.

I have inserted a diagram to help you understand how to break down long term goals until they become action plans or execution plans. You can also see the timelines of years, months and days.

Now, how would you know which goals you should start with? Yes, you need to focus on one, 2 goals at most, at a time. Yes, you will get exhausted if you choose to do too many things at once. Exhaustion causes people to feel overwhelmed, discouraged, and want to give up.

Here are my tips on how to choose a goal to start with:
- You can start with the most urgent goal.
- You can start with the most passionate goal.
- You can start with the easiest goal for you to accomplish.
- You can start with the goal that takes the shortest amount of time to complete.
- You can start with the most important goal for you.
- You can start with the goal that is most realistic for paying your bills.
- You can start with the goal that you can accomplish where you are presently in life.

80

- You can start with the goal that you can accomplish with what you have presently in life.
- You can start with the goal that you can afford to accomplish at the moment.
- You can start with the goal that will make the biggest impact on your life.

Once you choose your starting goals, you can start assigning a start and an end date to each one of them. Add them to your journals, planners, and schedules. Set reminders. Remember: what gets scheduled, gets done. Set up your daily routines and habits to align with your goals.

Now, I know that I've given you a lot of information. Amazing goal setting techniques started from the previous chapter. You might have gotten confused or lost track of the system along the way. I want to help you organize your thoughts.

I've designed a short, simple method for setting amazing goals:

1. Brainstorm - Assess every area of your life and list everything you would like to accomplish. Be bold! Challenge yourself. Set life goals. Check if your life goals are SMART.
2. Simplify - Group your similar life goals together to create fewer goals.
3. Prioritize - Look at your goals and work out a realistic timeline. Delegate your goals as long, medium, or short-term goals.
4. Action plan - Look at your short-term goals. Decide which goal you would like to work towards first. Be very specific: break your goals into objectives, a step-by-step plan so you can check on your progress.

After setting those amazing goals, you should regularly check in on your progress to make sure you're on the right path.

EVALUATE AND MONITOR YOUR PROGRESS

Regardless of your goal, whether your goal is to be promoted in the company where you work, create a business, have a healthy lifestyle, or study something new, evaluating your progress is a fundamental part of the process. Setting goals for yourself works; The problem is that many people tend to forget the effort required to achieve them since they set goals and then forget them. If you do not monitor and evaluate the progress, it will be difficult for you to progress, because you will not be aware of the path you have travelled. This is one of the main reasons people fail. If you are serious about your goals, you should always evaluate your progress.

When you evaluate your progress, you should track and measure them and you should be consciously connecting your goals to your life. In this way, you can actively progress towards reaching them. Because of this, you must make your goals measurably, focus on the main measure, and constantly monitor your progress to know what decisions and adjustments you need to make. As a result, you will know where you are, how to get there, and what you need to do immediately to move forward. When you are clear about the direction you are going, nothing can stop you.

Follow these tips to evaluate your progress:
1. Locate where you are and where you want to go
To achieve what you want in life, you must first know where you are and where you want to go. This can refer to any goal, for example, career goal, savings goal, or your dream job. Therefore, you must first measure your current and desired state. For example, if your goal is to save up to $400,000 in eighteen months, you should not just keep saving part of your salary every month but you should also evaluate how much you have been able to save in the past five months. You should ask yourself: have you been adhering to your monthly

saving goals? Will you be able to meet up with your deadline of eighteen months if you keep saving at this rate?

The above are the parameters to check to know if you are making progress by comparing where you are to where you are going.

2. Set a realistic time to reach your goal
You have to be realistic to reach the goal. If you set a very short time, you might feel unmotivated by not being able to achieve the goal in such a short time. However, if the time is too long, then there might not be any constant follow-up to get where you want to be.

In addition, you must break that period into even smaller periods. It is on these dates that you will evaluate your progress. Just like the example that I gave earlier, if your goal is to save up to $400,000 in eighteen months to start your dream business, you should check how much you have saved every week to closely monitor your progress. If your goal is to consistently save and watch your money grow, you should do a "cash cut-off" in which you can measure how much money you have been able to save.

3. Evaluate your level of discipline
Since you have deadlines and periods of evaluation, you must also be disciplined enough to stick to the plans that you have created to achieve your goals. You can have a structure that allows you to automate your progress. For example, working with the $400,000 savings goal, you can do the following:
- Have a weekly budget, that forms your overall monthly budget
- Buy all the things that you may need in advance for the whole week such as shaving sticks, detergent, food items, etc.

- Keep some money in case an unexpected circumstance shows up
- If you still have some money left after meeting up with the weekly saving goal, don't add it to savings and don't spend it lavishly, keep it till the next week. If the same happens at the end of the month, keep such savings till the following month.

With these tips, and especially the measurement of your progress, achieving your goals will be much easier. Once you start seeing the finish line, you will feel more motivated to push through to the end. Keep your motivation strong. You can!

CELEBRATE YOURSELF

Celebrating success is a personal thing. Among the most useful strategies, which I teach in my courses or personalized coaching sessions, is certainly that of celebrating successes. It's strange that very few do!

In fact, from an early age, I was taught to give greater importance to the things we do wrong or to those to be improved. As if it were unimportant to celebrate and emphasize the achievement of a goal or when another piece of a bigger goal is added to the big picture.

Success should never be taken for granted! That's why you have to celebrate it! To increasingly strengthen your confidence and self-esteem it is essential to celebrate yourself in every milestone of accomplishment as you draw closer to achieving your biggest goal. You can even do well to reward yourself for a good job done. You should celebrate with the same intensity that you put into achieving that goal.

At some points, you must have said to yourself "I'm wrong," "I didn't discipline myself very well on this," "It would have been better if I had..." Therefore, the need to always celebrate yourself when you got it right and accomplished your goal matters. Every time you symbolically celebrate a goal, either large or small, you nurture the sense of internal trust, the convictions of possibility and you add value to your personality.

"My goal is to build a life I do not need a vacation from." - Rob Hill Sr.

<u>CHAPTER SIX</u>

MY LIFESTYLE

Here comes the very last part. You have worked so hard to get to this point, and now you are just one chapter away from fully knowing how to build the life of your dreams, become your best self and live your life to the fullest. How do you feel so far? Yes, creating your best lifestyle is very important, but it is also important to live a lifestyle that is generally healthy and fulfilling. The previous chapters have been about how to create your best lifestyle. In this chapter, you'll learn how to become your best self and live your life to the fullest. You will learn lifestyle techniques to help you develop, keep and encourage your best lifestyle. I want to teach you how to navigate through life successfully while bringing your best self forward, bravely and unapologetically.

Your lifestyle is a set of attitudes and behaviours that you can adopt and develop to satisfy your basic needs as a human being, make yourself more effective and invest in your personal development. As you live your best lifestyle, you need to acquire skills that will assist you to navigate through life successfully so you always come out on top and stand out for the right reasons.

Some helpful skills to learn include:
- Accountability
- Tracking your goals
- Focus
- Finding motivation
- Overcoming self-doubt
- Eliminate fear of failure

- Embrace change
- Dealing with obstacles
- Developing competency
- Beating perfectionism
- Meditation
- Express gratitude

ACCOUNTABILITY

You are accountable for your life because you are the owner of your life and the person who has to live it. At the end of the day, it is your responsibility to give yourself your dream life. This is part of the reason you should only do things that you have genuine interest in. This way, you have no one else to blame if things don't work out but you feel proud when they do. It feels better to make a mistake through your own fault than someone else's.

When you write down your goals and plans to achieve them, you acquire a sense of personal accountability for their outcomes. When you share your goals with others, you create even more accountability, as you become answerable to more than one person. Having a support system is very encouraging to your success.

While it is important to be personally accountable, you can also receive support from the people in your life. These people could be your friends, social media, support groups, coach, etc. Have meet-ups, schedule meetings, celebrate with each other, share goals, make plans, and form other accountability strategies individually and collectively.

"A dream you dream alone is only a dream. A dream you dream together is reality."-John Lennon

TRACKING YOUR GOALS

Speaking of accountability, let's talk about how to track your life goals. First, as discussed in the previous chapter, you can identify your goals and create more clarity for your action plan by prioritizing them. Prioritizing your goals allows you to channel your focus on the top important goals. You can also break down your larger, key goals into smaller sub-goals or objectives. These might be stepwise milestones, or you might have an alternative pathway you would like to use instead but breaking down your goals allows you to plan better.

If you want to set deadlines or time frames for accomplishing each small sub-goal, it's fine. This adds another layer of personal accountability. It is commonly used in project management contexts. Set realistic, sufficiently challenging time frames because you'll also benefit from a healthy amount of pressure—eustress, in other words. When you have time-bound goals, you can better evaluate your progress. From there, you can adapt or adjust your generated pathways accordingly to maximize your chances of success. Goals can change, and sometimes how we achieve our goals can change, too. At that point, it becomes essential to keep brainstorming to generate new ideas for creating the ideal conditions that will support your goal pursuit.

Some ideas to keep you in line with your goals:
1. Brainstorm as many alternative pathways as you can. Think about all the potential ways you might go about achieving your goal. Don't be too quick to dismiss your ideas. Give your creative brain an exercise and record your ideas as you go. This will keep you from forgetting them later down the line.
2. Identify the resources you'll need. What is necessary for each step along the way? Then, what will make things easier

for you? Consider people who might support you as well as more tangible resources.

3. Plan out your progress if it helps. Think of motivation and accountability. Apply the eustress principle to the goal pursuit process rather than its outcomes. Use a planner, an app, or whatever else you find most valuable. Don't be afraid to adjust your pathway if it's necessary. Once you set your goals, you will need the motivation to keep going. As I have talked about in the previous chapter, intrinsic motivations are better motivators than extrinsic ones.

Remember

When your motivation is intrinsically driven, your likelihood of success increases. Intrinsic motivations are motivations that come from within you, which lead to your fulfilment. They are not motivations that come from wanting to please others, doing things just because you were asked to do them, or any other external factor. In other words, try to keep your motivations intrinsically driven. Get other people out of your head and dispose of other people's goals. Focus on your own goal.

FOCUS

Keep your eyes on the prize and focus on yourself. Focus on your vision. Focus, by definition, means to centre your interest or activity. In this journey of creating your best lifestyle, focus is a key factor that ensures progress. Without focus, you will become disengaged or discouraged.

Some signs that help you recognize you are losing your focus are:
- Getting easily distracted (by people, things, ideas, shiny objects, and so on).

- Always changing your mind, therefore changing course, and never staying on track. Working on things that are not generating results.

If you realize that you are losing your focus, use these steps to get back on track:

1. Write down all of the projects you currently have going on.
2. Order all the projects according to their deadlines.
3. Start with the one with the nearest deadline.
4. Commit to working on that project only until it is completed and successful.
5. After the first project is completed, you can start a new project by choosing the next one with the nearest deadline.

Once you've managed to keep yourself focused on your goal, you will stop making excuses, and finally, beat the evil that is called procrastination.

A reason you might lose focus, or interest, is because the goal that you are pursuing is not always pleasurable enough for you to do it. As humans, we are naturally accustomed to chasing pleasure and avoiding pain.

If this is the case for you, here are the two things you can do:

- Make the goal attractive to you. The goal needs to be enticing enough for you to pursue it. You can make your goal more attractive by adding attractive visual aids to your vision board. Another way to make your goals attractive is by rephrasing your goal statements. For example: Instead of saying "I want to lose 10 pounds," you can say "I want to be fit and healthy."

- Think of what you stand to gain if you pursue your goal, versus not pursuing your goal. That will motivate you to continue pursuing your goal.

FINDING MOTIVATION
So, how are you supposed to find motivation?

- Think of your motivational triggers and use them anytime you need a motivational boost. To identify your motivational triggers, think about things that empower you. They might be music, meditation, art, books, movies, magazines, serenity, documentaries, contributions, motivational speakers, dreams, places, people, exercise, information, progress, or happiness. Anytime you discover something that motivates you, take note of it so you can use it whenever you need motivation.
- Another method is to identify what demotivates you and avoid them. To identify what demotivates you, think about things that drain your energy. They might be food, bad habits, people, behaviours, places, organizations, etc. Discover your demotivators and take note of them too.

One factor that is essential to boost your motivation is learning how to overcome self-doubt.

OVERCOMING SELF-DOUBT
Self-doubt means having resistance to take desired actions. To overcome self-doubt, you need to first be able to recognize the signs of it.

These signs might look like this:

- Not going through with a plan because it is not perfect

- Making a plan and not acting on it
- Avoiding dealing with a situation
- Hesitation
- Hiding
- Behaving helpless

Once you recognize that you have signs of self-doubt, you can work on overcoming them.

I have some tips for you:

- Find out your self-doubting style and deal with it. For example, do you overthink when you do not want to do something? Do you hide? Do you get hyper-critical? What makes you feel helpless? How can you change these behaviours?
- Start small and take baby steps. You do not have to start with a big task because it might discourage you from beginning. Start by doing one small thing that will get you a step closer to your goal. Eventually, you should take more and bigger steps. Another way to take baby steps is to do the task on the side. For example, if you want to start a business but you are not sure of how it will go, you can start with a side hustle instead of quitting your day job right away.
- Develop self-love. When you look at the impact of not loving yourself, you will discover that it is working against you, not with you. Learn to love yourself and start doing more things that genuinely make you happy.
- Celebrate your progress. Tell yourself you did a good job. Reward yourself. Doing this creates momentum to do more things. It also makes you more self-reliant and confident.

- Use a planner. It will help you track and organize your goals.
- Remember why you want it. It will encourage you to do the task.
- Search for examples of other people who have done what you are trying to do, and imitate them.
- Take massive action. You can do something big that will leave you with no choice but to continue pursuing the rest of your goals!

ELIMINATE FEAR OF FAILURE

Just like self-doubt, you also have to eliminate your fear of failure. Your fear of failure might be the one main thing that is holding you back from pursuing your goals.

Some of the signs of fear of failure are:
- You don't want to take steps forward with putting yourself out there.
- You're scared of what other people might think
- When something goes wrong, you beat yourself up for days or weeks, and even wonder why you bother!

So how do you break away from this cycle? In order to eliminate fear of failure, you simply need to reframe your idea of failure, so you can feel encouraged that you're doing what it takes to be successful.

You can do this in several ways:
- Remind yourself whenever something goes wrong, "I don't fail, I only learn!"
- The next time something doesn't go as planned, write down 3 things you discovered, learned, or ways you benefited that you wouldn't have happened without the experience of failing.

- Understand that only a few things need to work to become successful, so keep the tally of wins and mistakes to remind yourself you're on track!

EMBRACE CHANGE

Along with eliminating your fears of failure, you should also embrace change. Here is a wake-up call for you, after this book, after all of these exercises, you will change. Change is an inevitable part of life. Resisting change will only hurt you in the long run.

There is a pattern to resisting change. It looks something like this:

1. Discontent: You're unhappy with your life but you're there because it's comfortable and familiar.
2. Breaking point: You're getting fed up with your cycle.
3. Decision: You decide and declare that you will change. You take that first step.
4. Fear: You become uncomfortable and anxious. You start doubting your decision to change.
5. Amnesia: Your fear makes your original lifestyle look better because you're used to it, it's comfortable and familiar. You forget why you wanted to change in the first place.
6. Backtracking: You decide to go back to your old lifestyle.

If you keep backtracking, one of the 2 things are bound to happen to you:

1. Extreme circumstance: A situation will happen to you that will push you to evolve.
2. Self-honesty: You receive a breakthrough. You admit the truth to yourself. You learn something new about your situation.

Welcoming change will prevent you from being a victim to life's circumstances, and help keep you on top no matter the circumstance.

Some benefits of embracing changes are:
1. They create opportunities and possibilities
2. They are learning opportunities
3. They make you more resilient
4. They encourage you to be proactive
5. They make life more interesting

DEALING WITH OBSTACLES

Living your best lifestyle is a life journey, and life isn't always a breeze. As you live, you are bound to come across obstacles that come with life. An obstacle is a thing that blocks one's way, prevents or hinders progress. Obstacles are inevitable simply because they are part of life. You are bound to run into at least one factor that might hold you back from living your best lifestyle at any moment. This does not mean that you should give up. Remember that everything in life has obstacles. To always live your best lifestyle, you must learn to deal with these setbacks in the best way possible.

Here are some of my tips to keep you living your best lifestyle, even when you come across obstacles along the way:
1. Plan for unlikely obstacles, expect the unexpected. Part of being sensible means planning for possibilities. Consider these events: What might prevent you from pursuing one pathway and encourage you onto another? How might you keep away from or conquer hindrances through proactive planning?
2. Utilize positive self-talk. As you may have discovered from chapter 2, your self-talk is pretty powerful. Hope

is very important and positive self-talk assumes a key job in conquering hindrances. Planning proactively for negative scenarios helps counter negative self-talk. Meanwhile, your sense of self-efficacy is a vital factor in goal achievement.

3. Develop resilience. Difficulties can incur significant damage and lead to loss of interest. You can simply build up your ability to manage difficulties through resilience training and exercises.
4. Assess your advancement. Your needs may change en route, so assessment is not really about progress or disappointment. You can adjust your goals by making them more or less challenging, or change their inclinations as you see fit.

DEVELOPING COMPETENCY

Another helpful skill is to develop your sense of competency. Competency means assessing the skills needed for a task and making sure you are prepared for the task, otherwise, acquiring the knowledge or skill to achieve the task.

Here are some tips to develop competency:

1. Believe that you can achieve your goal with a growth mindset.
2. Find out what you need to do to achieve your goal.
3. Take steps towards achieving your goal. If you need to start taking classes, practicing a behavior, etc, start doing it!
4. Practice makes perfect. Get as much practice as you can.

Although practice makes perfect, you shouldn't rely on perfect. I'll tell you why.

BEATING PERFECTIONISM

Perfectionism means waiting for a thing to be perfect enough to finally move forward. The problem with this style of thinking is that the perfect time or condition never fully exists. A perfectionist mindset is a problem because it holds you back. It is completely understandable why you would want to present yourself in the best way possible but this attitude can very easily turn into a form of procrastination because 'perfect' is an unachievable state. Choose done over perfect. Keep in mind that things only need to be good enough to be presentable. If you continue making changes, it will never be good enough for you.

Some signs that you are in a cycle of perfectionism might be:
- Over-thinking things and feeling like you need to get everything "just right" before you present anything or move forward.
- Needing to comprehend everything before making a move.
- You have too many half-assembled projects.

Some techniques to help you beat perfectionism are:
- Place strict deadlines and reminders on projects that will force you to take action.
- Avoid jumping from project to project, leaving half-built assignments. Instead, focus on one task at a time and see it to completion before starting a new task.

Tip: If you feel like you are starting to head down the perfectionist route when creating something, remember 2 things:
1. Good is good enough
2. Done is better than perfect

MEDITATION

Meditation is a practice where a person focuses their mind on a particular object, thought, or activity to train attention and awareness, and achieve a mentally clear and emotionally calm and stable state.

Meditation is similar to mindfulness. Mindfulness is the ability to be present, to rest in the here and now, fully engaged with whatever we're doing in the moment. Meditation is common in a lot of religious practices, like praying.

Some benefits of meditation are:
- It reduces stress and anxiety
- It increases attention span
- It makes you more self-aware
- It encourages you to gain more control of your thoughts and feelings
- It reduces memory loss
- It helps control pain
- It improves sleep

An easy but effective way to meditate is to simply focus on your breathing. Try this: stop what you're doing and focus on breathing in and breathing out. Closing your eyes helps. As you do this, your mind might wander, especially when you're new to meditation. This is completely natural. Your duty is to gently bring your mind back to your breathing.

Guided meditation is a form of meditation. It means listening to a recording that gives relaxation ideas or sounds. All you have to do is listen to them and follow instructions, as you meditate.

EXPRESS GRATITUDE

Gratitude is the quality of being thankful; readiness to show appreciation for and to return kindness. Gratitude or gratefulness comes from the Latin word gratus meaning "pleasing, thankful." It is a feeling of appreciation felt by and/or similar positive response shown by the recipient of kindness, gifts, help, favors, or other types of generosity, towards the giver of such gifts.

It's easy to become too focused, and even obsessed with achieving goals and major life changes. This can lead to unhappiness and frustration, especially if the goal takes much longer than you intended. This is where gratitude comes into the picture.

Some benefits of gratitude are:
- It makes you happier
- It increases positive emotions
- It makes people like you
- It increases self-esteem
- It strengthens relationships
- It makes you kinder
- It makes you less shallow
- It reduces depression
- It reduces impatience
- It improves improve decision-making

Take a few minutes to be grateful for what you already have. Write all the things you're grateful for and that you appreciate. You can create a gratitude journal, then answer gratitude prompts or list the things that you're grateful for each day. Gratitude doesn't have to be big things. You should be grateful for simple things such as having enough food, good health, a safe and comfortable place to live or enough money. Be grateful for waking up and experiencing another day of your life. Remember that something that has little value to you might be of great significance to someone else. That's a reason to be grateful.

Now that you have developed the skills for a successful life, you have to live your life confidently by presenting your best self at all times.

Activities to keep you at your best self:
- Self-confidence
- Social confidence
- Effective communication
- Self-awareness and self-acceptance
- Self-care and self-love
- Journaling for self-care
- Productive Habits
- Invest in yourself

SELF-CONFIDENCE
Confidence simply means a feeling of trust in one's abilities, qualities, and judgment. It's a vital step in presenting your best self to the world and living your best lifestyle because it makes a big difference in your presentation and the way you're perceived by others. Being confident has many benefits, such as looking smarter, being more articulate, more successful, and more trustworthy to name a few.

Signs of lack of self-confidence:
- Hiding
- Fear or anxiety
- Agreeing to or accepting things you're not comfortable with
- Approval-seeking

- Lowering your standards
- Being a pushover
- Trusting other people's judgment over your own
- Have too few boundaries

Here are some tips for developing self-confidence:
- Understand your strengths
- Face your fears
- Learn how to communicate properly
- Practice positive thinking
- Practice expressional skills
- Develop competency
- Take risks
- Practice good posture
- Try new things
- Challenge yourself

SOCIAL CONFIDENCE

Another step to get the most out of your life is by developing social confidence. Being confident in who you are is one thing but being socially confident is a different thing. Social confidence means being able to carry yourself well around people.

Here are my suggestions to develop social confidence:
- Identify the situation and know your role. If you are the leader, act like it. If you are an audience member, act as an audience member. Act appropriately according to the event.
- Develop self-love. Get to know yourself and love yourself. Use your strengths. Do not participate in things that do not encourage your growth or progress. Nobody should make you feel inferior or force you to do things that you do not want to do.

101

- Be prepared. Do your research on the things that you need before attending the social occasion and come prepared. This will help you to feel confident.
- Emulate the traits that you like about other people into your own life. Ask yourself, "What do I like about this person?" "Is that a trait I want to develop?" If yes, "What are the steps to developing that trait?"

EFFECTIVE COMMUNICATION

To increase your confidence, you should develop your expressional skills, as they will expand your comfort zone since being able to make your points effectively is a great way to boost confidence.

Some techniques for effective communication are:
- Make your statements about yourself and how you feel. Use the word "I." For example, "I feel that you do not care." Another one is "This is what I like about you."
- Make exact statements. Give proper descriptions. It helps you become specific, therefore making your point clear. For example, "I don't want that."
- Say positive things first before telling bitter truths. It makes people feel better and accept their errors easier. For example, you can say "Although I agree with what you said, I do not agree with the way you said it."
- Validate your expressions. A way of doing this is to state how you feel and what makes you feel that way. Give supporting evidence if available.
- Use proper body language. You might be surprised to know that a large part of the message you communicate to others do not come from your

speech but they come from your body language and tone.

- Use proper tone and pace when you speak. Do not be rude, mean, aggressive, loud, too quiet, too fast, etc. Try to sound clear, articulate and firm.

SELF-AWARENESS AND SELF-ACCEPTANCE

Building confidence comes from being self-aware. In the broadest sense, self-awareness means having a deep understanding of your whole being, this means your values, strengths, weaknesses, habits, and your "why." Along with getting to know yourself, you should accept yourself for who you truly are, including your faults. When you accept your challenges, you become focused on different strategies for self-improvement. Don't be afraid to get to know who you are. Doing so will help you make decisions that are best suited for you.

Self-awareness is the vital first step in mastering your strengths, taking control of your life, and creating your future. Where you choose to focus your energy, emotions, strengths, and reactions plays a major role in where you will end up in life. Self-awareness helps you understand your desires better so recalibrate yourself, your needs, your wants according to your true self.

Below are some of my tips to become more self-aware:
- Observe yourself objectively
- Keep a journal
- Write down your goals, plans, and priorities
- Perform daily self-reflection
- Practice meditation and other mindfulness habits
- Take personality and psychometric tests
- Ask trusted friends to describe you

- Ask for feedback

Some techniques to assists you with accepting yourself are as follows:
- Embrace what makes you unique
- Let go of the things you cannot change
- Identify your strengths
- Challenge yourself
- Celebrate your accomplishments
- Prepare ahead for things you're not best at
- Think positively
- Be kind to yourself
- Find support
- Practice self-love

SELF CARE AND SELF-LOVE
Possibly the biggest way to eliminate burnout is practicing self-care. Self-care means simply taking care of yourself. Self-love is exactly what it sounds like, loving yourself. When you have these traits, you will value yourself and make yourself a priority. You cannot pour from an empty cup. You have to show care and love to yourself first before you can give yourself to the world.

Self-care and self-love activities can be a wide variety of things. They can be physical, emotional, mental, and spiritual. They can be big, full rituals that take a lot of your time, they can be the smallest things like lighting a candle while working, or they can fall in between.

Here are some ideas to help you love and care for yourself:
- Get enough sleep
- Exercise regularly
- Eat a healthy, balanced diet

- Drink plenty of water
- Avoid alcohol
- Read more
- Go for medical visits
- Be mindful and meditative
- Show appreciation
- Be kind
- Keep a journal
- Make time for loved ones
- Take care of your appearance
- See a life coach, counsellor, or psychiatrist
- Detox (digital detox, body cleanse, etc.)
- Do more of the things you love
- Practice forgiveness
- Celebrate your accomplishments
- Try the things you have always wanted to do
- Reflect on your day
- Use positive language and self-talk
- Set new goals
- Declutter
- Get to know yourself
- Choose what you spend your time on wisely
- Pray
- Decorate your home with plants
- Use essential oils
- Listen to music that makes you feel good
- Spend time in nature
- Take supplements for nutrients
- Surround yourself with positive people

JOURNALING FOR SELF-CARE

If you haven't noticed already, I am a big advocate of journaling. I believe it is an essential tool for understanding yourself, for keeping your thoughts in one place other than inside of your brain, and an essential part of self-care. A journal is a book of notes written by you, to you. Journaling can be a form of self-therapy, guidance, organizer, reminder, tracker, or anything else you want it to serve. It just depends on how you use it. For some people, a journal serves as all of the above, and for some others, they would rather have a different journal for each purpose. Either way, journals are very useful for personal and professional development.

If you haven't started journaling already, here's how to start a journal:

1. Buy an inspirational notebook or tool for writing. Decide if you enjoy handwriting your thoughts and feelings or if you prefer it in a digital format. Some people think that handwriting your ideas as you self-reflect has a more meaningful impact, while others prefer the quick access of a digital format. Choose whichever method is easier for you to practice.

2. Pick a time. Schedule a time to journal each day. Also, create a routine so you develop a sense of consistency. Mornings and evenings are often effective times to journal (you can start the day in a positive space or finish it by reflecting on uplifting parts).

3. Find a place. Ideally, pick a place that is quiet and has an atmosphere of solitude and peace. This might be a quiet corner of your home, a favourite coffee shop, or even outdoors in nature.

4. Set a timer. Since one of the most significant obstacles to journaling is time, start small. Set a timer for 10 minutes. You will be amazed at what can happen in just ten minutes a day.

5. Select a prompt. Have a list of prompts ready, so you have direction. There are endless lists of prompts that will help alleviate boredom and keep you motivated everyday.

PRODUCTIVE HABITS
Creating productive habits for yourself will definitely add more value to your life. As the name suggests, the habits have to be productive. They have to add some type of value to you, no matter how small or slow. Adopt habits that will help you achieve a more prosperous life.

Some recommendations of productive habits are:
- Read
- Journal
- Wake up early
- Take criticism constructively
- Reflect and visualize
- Prioritize
- Be a life-long learner
- Make sure you always show up to all your obligations
- Be hardworking
- Have lifestyle routines (morning routine, night-time routines, etc)
- Make to-do lists
- Practice self-care
- Live below your means
- Be a good listener
- Take responsibility for your actions
- Take control of your finances
- Take reasonable risks
- Be punctual
- Save energy whenever possible
- Take responsibility for your actions
- Keep an organized space

- Educate yourself daily
- Budget and track your expenses
- Stop procrastinating
- Always keep your words

Did you know this?
Studies suggest that it takes 21 days to form a new habit. Also, when you add a new habit to an old one, it is more likely to stick with you.

Along with developing new habits, you should stop existing bad habits and stay away from habits that do not bring out the best in you. Think of those habits that don't support your best lifestyle and make a commitment to stop them for good. Then, think of new habits that you want to adopt.

To create a new habit, you can use this method called "The 3 Rs of habit change":

- Reminder (the trigger that initiates the behaviour)- Set a reminder for your new habit
- Routine (the behaviour itself; the action you take)- Choose a habit that is easy to start
- Reward (the benefit you gain from doing the behaviour)- Choose your reward

"Success does not come from what you do occasionally, it comes from what you do consistently." -Marie Forleo

INVEST IN YOURSELF
To always be your best self, one of the habits to develop is becoming a lifelong learner. Always seek personal growth and ways to transform yourself. This habit doesn't mean that you're not already great, it just means that you want to be better. There's nothing wrong with that. Also, if you need

assistance with something, you should seek help. Do not feel embarrassed. See it as an investment in your personal development. You should only invest yourself, your time, and your energy into things that add value to you.

An investment in yourself can never go to waste because it stays with you forever, and allows room for new opportunities. The more you invest in something, the more it becomes your identity.

"Ultimately, there is one investment that supersedes all others: Invest in yourself. Nobody can take away what you have got in yourself, and everybody has potential they have not used yet." -Warren Buffet

Some ways you can invest in yourself:
- Learn a new skill
- Travel
- Take a class or workshop
- Read, watch and listen
- Hire a coach
- Have a mentor
- Start a business or side hustle
- Prioritize self-care
- Monitor your health and wellness
- Learn to cook
- Make plans and set goals
- Network
- Learn a new language
- Manage your time better
- Save your money
- Invest your money
- Take on new challenges

You can design a worksheet like this to get you started:

A healthy lifestyle is perhaps the purpose that we all in some way or another pursue every day, for which we often make small but significant transformations in our daily lives, and with which we try to stay connected despite the eagerness that sometimes seems to interrupt our days. But how conscious do we really assume this will be in our lives?

MAINTAIN A HEALTHY LIFESTYLE

This chapter would not be complete without taking a look at how to maintain a healthy lifestyle. How long and how well you will live depends on your health. It is natural that you adopt healthy habits and therefore a healthy lifestyle, your body can benefit from it. You probably continuously hear about the importance of living a better, healthier lifestyle, but you might not know how to do it or what makes it so necessary. This ignorance is more common with young people.

A healthy lifestyle is not only about special food or exercise. A healthy lifestyle consists of a whole range of measures aimed at improving health and preventing pathological processes in the body. Compliance with the rules of a healthy lifestyle can significantly increase life expectancy while improving its quality. To achieve a healthy lifestyle, it is necessary to take into account your health in a holistic way, because this way, you will enjoy a fuller existence.

HEALTHY LIFESTYLE HABITS
Creating a healthy lifestyle habit is not a single activity that you have to do, nor is there only a single space where you can apply it. In an integral concept, they are, as their name says, habits that you should incorporate in each element of your daily context. Including as many healthy habits as positive will allow you to develop increased well-being for your body and your mind. Some of these habits are so simple that sometimes you probably overlook them. For example, getting up a little earlier than necessary to create more complete routines in your mornings, and taking away a little stress at the beginning of your day might seem unnecessary to some people.

From another perspective, not all habits are for all people. Deciding to not make use of any of the suggestions does not mean that you do not have a balanced, healthy lifestyle. You must establish customs that fit you, your personality, and your needs. For some people, certain activities can be relaxing, while for others, they can be seen as a situation that causes anxiety. Do not participate in uncomfortable habits simply because you're trying to fit. You should look for those habits that provide you with better moments.

FUNDAMENTALS AND METHODS OF FORMING A HEALTHY LIFESTYLE

A healthy lifestyle has 7 main pillars: physical activity, balanced nutrition, absence of bad habits, hygienic care, good sleep and rest, wellness procedures, and emotional mood. If you follow all these recommendations, the quality of your life and well-being will significantly improve.

Compliance with proper nutrition

The health of internal organs, appearance, well-being, and immunity directly depends on what you eat. A healthy lifestyle involves eliminating or at least reducing flavors, flavour enhancers, fatty foods, and preservatives.

Here are some basic eating rules:

- You should not starve or overeat. Both of them negatively affect your well-being. You can't feel hungry and, conversely, overeat. Try to ensure that your daily calorie intake is 1700-1900 kcal (the norm for women leading a sedentary lifestyle). For men, the daily calorie intake is about 300-400 kcal higher.
- Drink clean water. It is advisable for every adult to consume from 1.5 to 2 litres of water per day (does not include tea, coffee, juice, etc.)
- Cut back on sweets in your diet. If you want something sweet, give preference to fresh vegetables or dried fruits. You can also consume dark chocolate in moderation.
- Eat between 4-5 small meals a day. At the end of each meal, there should be a feeling of slight hunger.
- Your daily menu should include meat or fish, vegetables and fruits, cereals, dairy products. Eat a variety of foods, unless you're a vegetarian.

- It is advisable to have dinner at least 2 hours before bedtime. It is undesirable to eat immediately before bedtime.
- Eliminate fast food, fatty, and smoked foods from your diet.
- Give preference to cooking, stewing, or baking food, instead of dining out.

If you have not followed a diet before, it can be difficult for you to make drastic changes in your eating habits. Try to start small by reducing fatty sauces and foods that contain them, avoid flavour enhancers and chemical additives in food, give up instant foods, convenience foods, confectionery, and increase the proportion of fruits and vegetables in your menu. Completing each of these steps will be a step towards a healthy diet.

Physical activity

Lack of physical activity leads to a decrease in the metabolic rate, and the development of diseases in the musculoskeletal system, cardiovascular and neurological pathologies.

If your job does not invoke movement, try to increase your activity yourself. It is considered normal to be in motion for at least 1 hour a day (this is about 8000-10,000 steps). Scientists have proven that every minute of activity positively affects the state of the body in the long term; which means that even climbing stairs, rather than taking an elevator, already brings you closer to good health.

You can increase your daily activity by making it a habit to start and end your day with a gentle warm-up. If you go to work by public transport, get off 1-2 stops earlier and walk this path. Taking breaks is very helpful if you have a sedentary job. Get some fitness, go for a walk or the pool on weekends. These measures are sufficient to maintain health and wellness.

Hygienic care
Personal hygiene is one of the components of a healthy lifestyle. This primarily concerns the oral cavity. You need to brush your teeth at least twice a day and pay attention to your entire oral cavity. In addition to the standard set of toothbrushes and toothpaste, get an irrigator, dental floss, and mouthwash. Failure to comply with these rules is fraught not only with the development of cavities but also with the threat of the development of periodontitis and diseases of the gastrointestinal tract.

It is also important to keep your home in order: regularly perform wet cleaning, prevent the accumulation of dust, and ventilate the rooms daily.

Sleep and rest well
Scientists have concluded that sleep duration and regularity are important for health and wellness. Everyone should sleep up to 8 hours a day. Of course, sometimes you can make exceptions, for example, on weekends.

Even if you hear it a lot and believe that everything is relative, sleep is an essential activity for our body. Do not underestimate it. 8 hours of sleep is essential for your well-being. Create a habit of going to bed at a certain time, as well as getting up from bed at a certain time.

Emotional attitude
Nervous tensions, constant breakdowns, stress - all this negatively affects mood, well-being, and health in general. Experts recommend adhering to the following tips:

- Don't worry about what you can't change. If you cannot cope with anxiety, seek help from a psychologist.
- Think positively, find the silver lining in every situation.
- Do not hold evil, let go of all insults, do not envy and do not harm people.
- Try to avoid stressful situations.

Quitting bad habits (smoking, alcohol, drugs)

When smoking, colds and coughs are more likely to lead to complications. The smoker does not inhale all the harmful substances in tobacco smoke - about half goes to those who are near him. In families of smokers, children suffer from respiratory diseases much more often than in families where no one smokes. Continuous and prolonged smoking leads to premature aging. Limit your alcohol intake. Alcoholism has a destructive effect on all human systems and organs. The change in the psyche that occurs during episodic intake of alcohol (agitation, depression, etc.) determines the frequency of suicides committed in a state of intoxication.

Harmonious relationships with others

Keep a circle of close, trusted friends. Stay in touch with your family members. Try to live a life that includes healthy interactions with others. Cut off people with toxic energy from your personal space. Learn and practice the art of proper communication. Don't force yourself to become somebody you're not in an effort to please others.

Other recommendations

Both before sleeping and when waking up, it is not a good idea to use your cell phone. We know that there is much stimulation in it that can cause sleep problems, so it is not recommended that it be our partner before sleeping. On the other hand, when we wake up, out of habit, we take it and start another series of simulations, which somehow break the peace with which we can start the day. If it fits into your mornings, some recommend meditating, some just sit quietly, for others reading may be an option, or listening to music. A very common recommendation is to start the day with a glass of warm water with lemon juice.

CONCLUSION

FINAL THOUGHTS

Y ou have successfully completed this book. I'm personally very proud of you because you have taken a great step forward towards building a great life. This is a milestone worthy of celebration. From reading this book, I'm sure you now have a perfect understanding of what living your best lifestyle is about.

I want to recap some of the highlights of this book. I told you about what it means to live your best lifestyle and why you should live your dream life. I told you my story. I told you about life's purpose: what it is, why you should find yours and how to find yours. Then, I told you why having a positive and abundant mindset is encouraging to your success in life, how to deal with your limiting beliefs, and ways to develop a positive thinking and growth mindset. After that, I helped you build your vision. I also told you about the key different manifestation techniques of achieving your best lifestyle, which were vision boarding, the law of attraction, and affirmations. Then I got you to design every area of your dream life. I gave you some life categories and told you to decide what you wanted for each category to ensure that you set goals that made you satisfied on every level of your life. Once you got a grasp of exactly what you wanted for every area of your life, you started setting goals for yourself to achieve them. I told you how to set effective goals. Then I told you how to set SMART goals, classify your goals as short, medium, or long-term goals, prioritize your goals and set action plans to begin your goals today. In the final chapter, I gave you different techniques to help you navigate through life successfully. I told you ways to track your goals, maintain motivation, focus, etc. I also told you how to develop confidence, self-awareness, self-care, and more.

This book is a guide, a helping tool for you as you build and maintain your very best lifestyle. You don't need to put this book away after reading it once. You can read this book numerous times and share it with your loved ones. Everyone should live their best lifestyle because it makes the world a better place.

Now that you know how to live your best lifestyle, you're going to transform your life into something incredible. Get ready to be the envy of people's eyes. People will wonder how you became so perfect. The question is: apart from having a great life, what will you do with your newfound wisdom? Don't just live your best lifestyle, take yourself to your next level of greatness.

Here are some ways you can take yourself to the next level:
- Be a role model. Carry yourself in a profound way. Become someone people look up to when they want to find the way forward.
- Help others. Help those in need of what you have. You can help in any way that you can.
- Mentoring. You can become a mentor to people that also want to live their best lifestyles.
- Build your legacy. Think of what you want to be remembered for when you die and start building it. Leave a positive feeling with everyone you meet because people remember how you made them feel more than what you did or said.
- Raise the next generation to live their best lifestyles. Living your best lifestyle doesn't have to end with you. You can encourage your children to start from a

young age by teaching them about some of the tools and techniques you've learned. They can start keeping a journal from a young age like I did.

One last quote to remember: Life is about the journey, not the result. Make the most of this amazing journey. Always remember to enjoy the journey of life.

Made in the USA
Monee, IL
22 July 2022